LEWIS & CLARK EXPEDITION

ILLUSTRATED GLOSSARY

by Barbara Fifer

For Stan Fifer—father, friend, and the newspaperman who taught me how to write a lead.

Acknowledgments

For vetting the text and advising where dangers lay, many thanks to Stephen Witte. For designing an inviting layout while coping with text changes, much appreciation to Bob Smith. For their assiduous proofreading, relieved thanks to Joann Horner and Lisa Juvik. For research guidance and general support, profound gratitude to Joseph E. Mussulman, Kathryn Otto, and Dave Walter.

Notes on the text

Cross-references between entries are printed in LARGE AND SMALL CAPITAL LETTERS. Because the names of Meriwether Lewis and William Clark, appear so often, these are printed in standard upper-case and lower-case style throughout.

For ease of reading, modern place names are used; space limitations do not always permit qualifiers like "future," or "what would become." During the expedition, Ohio was the westernmost state of the United States, Indiana was still a territory, and Missouri had not yet become a territory.

Quotations, using the men's original spelling, capitalization, punctuation, and grammar, are taken from Gary E. Moulton, editor, *The Journals of the Lewis & Clark Expedition,* Volumes 2-11, published by University of Nebraska Press (1986-1997).

COVER IMAGES COURTESY OF (CLOCKWISE FROM UPPER LEFT): J. AGEE, BOB EVERTON, LARKSPUR BOOKS/A. SCOTT EARLE, CAHOKIA COURTHOUSE STATE HISTORIC SITE, J. AGEE, DONALD M. JONES, JEFFERSON NATIONAL EXPANSION MEMORIAL/NATIONAL PARK SERVICE, MONTANA MAGAZINE, GEORGE WUERTHNER, LIBRARY OF CONGRESS, J. AGEE.

ISBN 1-56037-227-3

Library of Congress Control Number: 2002096440

© 2003 Farcountry Press

Photographs © by individual photographers as credited

Created, designed, and published in the USA. Printed in Korea.

ague Any illness whose symptoms include chills and fever. One such sickness that affected the Corps of Discovery was MALARIA.

air gun *See* GUNS.

altitude When the captains used the term, they meant positions of celestial bodies, in degrees above the horizon. They had no way to measure altitude from sea level, which is commonly called "elevation." When they reached FORT MANDAN in November 1804 (elevation 1,701'), Lewis had climbed 1,656' from 45' above sea level at Philadelphia in 1803.

BOB EVERTON

anchovy (eulachon; *Thaleichthys pacificus*) What Lewis called the candle fish. The small fish that ran upstream on the COLUMBIA RIVER in the spring was welcomed into the Corps' diet beginning February 24, 1806, when Lewis wrote the first scientific description and sketched the fish.

Arikara Indians In 1804, enemies of the MANDAN AND HIDATSA INDIANS who made peace with them through the captains, and then broke the treaty before 1806. They prevented Chief SHEHEKE's timely return home after the expedition. Today the Arikara, Hidatsa, and Mandan form the Three Affiliated Tribes of Fort Berthold Indian Reservation, North Dakota.

artificial horizon A spirit (liquid-filled) level, used with the SEXTANT when the natural horizon could not be seen. Andrew ELLICOTT developed an improved version for Lewis in 1803, taking into mind the rough, mountainous terrain the Corps expected to travel.

Assiniboine Indians A Siouan tribe that broke off from the Yanktons before white contact in 1640. They then lived in what became Ontario, Canada. By 1804-1805, they lived northwest of the MANDAN AND HIDATSA INDIANS, where they both raided and traded. Today they share Fort Peck Indian Reservation in Montana with the GROS VENTRES INDIANS. It borders the MISSOURI RIVER east of Fort Peck Lake.

Audubon bighorn sheep *See* SHEEP, BIGHORN.

azimuth Compass bearing, written in degrees, that records the exact direction between two points. Degrees are read clockwise, with North being 0°. See also CIRCUMFERENTOR.

badger (*Taxidea taxus*) The animal was known in Europe and had been recorded in Canada but not in the future United States. Lewis killed and preserved one on July 30, 1804, near today's Fort Calhoun, Nebraska. Lewis and JEFFERSON both thought theirs was the first North American specimen.

badger
DONALD M. JONES

barge The captains' occasional term for their KEELBOAT.

barks, the See PERUVIAN BARK.

barking squirrel The captains' term for the PRAIRIE DOG.

Barton, Benjamin Smith (1766-1818) Lewis's journals often refer to obtaining botanical specimens for "Dr. Barton," natural history and botany professor at future University of Pennsylvania in PHILADELPHIA. In the summer of 1803, Barton taught Lewis the proper way to gather and preserve plant specimens, and how to describe them in writing. He also had written the United States' first botany textbook, and Lewis took along a copy. After the expedition, Barton was to write a book holding Lewis's botanical observations, but it never came about.

Beacon Rock Today rises about 840' on the COLUMBIA RIVER'S Washington shore west of North Bonneville. First reached and named by Clark on October 31, 1805. The Corps camped by it on November 2, 1805, and passed it on the homeward trip on April 6, 1806. Lewis noted in the spring that the river, swollen with snow melt, was 12' higher on the rock than it had been the previous fall. The name was lost from 1811, when an Astor fur company expedition named it Inoshoack Castle, which became Castle Rock until 1916, when "Beacon" was restored by the United States Board of Geographic Names. The eroded volcanic plug is protected in Beacon Rock State Park.

Beacon Rock
FRED PFLUGHOFT

beads An important trade item for nations that did not have glass-making technology. In PHILADELPHIA, Lewis bought strung beads by the pound. On the trek, he measured them out by the BRACE for trading or giving. Lewis purchased thirty-three and one quarter pounds of beads (of which eight and a half pounds were red). On May 13, 1806, he wrote that blue beads—the favorite color—"may be justly compared to goald or silver" in trading value. The Corps unfortunately ran out of blue beads, and ran low on other colors before heading home. On April 24, 1806, the captains sold CANOES to some Indians for beads to replenish their trading stock.

J. AGEE

bear, black (*Ursus americanus*) Smaller and less ferocious than the grizzly (*see* BEAR, GRIZZLY), these animals were familiar to the Corps, and lived around CAMP DUBOIS in Illinois. Black bears do not have the white-tipped fur of grizzlies, but, like grizzlies, range in color from light to dark. At FORT MANDAN, the captains heard about "red" bears in the country ahead, which is now assumed to be black bears in their cinnamon phase.

bear, grizzly (*Ursus horribilis*) The captains often called the grizzly bear "white bear," from the appearance of its fur. It ranges in color from blond to dark brown, and is tipped with white. The animals are about six or seven feet long, and three and a half or more feet high at the shoulder, with curved claws about four inches long. Unlike black bears, they have dished faces and humps over the shoulders. Grizzlies are omnivores, eating meat, fruit, grasses, and insects. They dig dens in the ground or enter caves to sleep but not truly hibernate during winter. Once at home on the PRAIRIE, grizzlies now survive in the contiguous 48 states only in remote mountain areas of the Northern Rockies.

grizzly bear
BOB EVERTON

Clark saw the first grizzly bear track on October 7, 1804, near today's Mobridge, South Dakota. Thirteen days later, CRUZATTE shot one; wounded, it charged him and he dropped his gun and ran. The bear escaped.

On April 29, 1805, Lewis and another man jointly shot the Corps' first grizzly bear specimen in future Roosevelt County, Montana. Wounded, it charged Lewis for 70 or 80 yards before both men fired again and brought it down. Lewis then measured it and wrote the first scientific description of the species.

Besides eating the meat, the Corps rendered oil or "bear grease" for cooking—and for smearing on their own skin as a MOSQUITO repellent.

black bear
DONALD M. JONES

bearberry *See* BERRIES.

Beaten Rock *See* BEACON ROCK.

beaver *(Castor canadensis)* American beaver. A large rodent that lives in streams, it grows to about 3' to 4' in length and 60 pounds. The well known animal had been trapped for its fur in North America since the late 17th century, but the Lewis and Clark Expedition occurred just as the MISSOURI RIVER fur trade was opening. The Corps saw their first beavers in future Atchison County, Kansas, on July 3, 1804. The captains noted that the pelts of the Upper Missouri River's beavers were the finest they had ever seen. DROUILLARD carried along some beaver traps, which he regularly set; the men also shot beavers, and SEAMAN retrieved them. The Corps considered the beaver's wide, flat tail a delicacy, and it was big enough to make a meal for two hungry men. When Clark's party was following the East Gallatin River in July 1806 near Bozeman, Montana, beaver-built lodges, dams, and ponds were everywhere, creating many detours.

American beaver with old tail injury
DONALD M. JONES

beaver, mountain *(Aplodontia rufa)* On February 26, 1806, Lewis wrote about his frustration at not being able to make Indian neighbors understand that he wanted

mountain beaver
BOB EVERTON

a specimen of the entire creature. A tail-less primitive rodent, not a BEAVER, it has silky hair that Indians left on the hides, which made a "very pleasant light lining" for garments made of Oregon bobcat. Lewis wrongly thought that the creature—which he never did see—might be related to weasels and minks.

Beaverhead Mountains Southern portion of the BITTERROOT RANGE of the ROCKY MOUNTAINS. On today's Idaho-Montana border, they trend southeast beginning roughly east of Gibbonsville, Idaho. See also LEMHI PASS.

Beaverhead River In Montana, the tributary of the JEFFERSON RIVER that the captains followed upstream looking for the CONTINENTAL DIVIDE in August 1805. To them it was still the Jefferson River, which today is considered to begin after the Ruby River and Big Hole River join the Beaverhead at Twin Bridges, Montana.

Beaverhead Rock
JOHN LAMBING

Beaverhead Rock Limestone monolith that rises 370' above its base elevation of 4,949'. On August 8, 1805, SACAGAWEA recognized this landmark in the area where her people spent summers. She told the captains that the SHOSHONE INDIANS called it "the beaver's head" because it resembled that part of a swimming BEAVER'S profile. Even better, she also said they would soon meet the Shoshones, either here on the BEAVERHEAD RIVER, or on the next river to its west. Today Beaverhead Rock is in the undeveloped Beaverhead Rock State Park between Twin Bridges and Dillon, Montana.

berries Wild berries were used by Indian nations both fresh and preserved. The same was true for the Lewis and Clark Expedition. A few types they described that were new to science are:

bearberry (Arctostaphylos uva-ursi) Kinnikinnick. Bright red, mealy, bland-tasting fruit that was cooked with meat or meat fat.

buffalo berry (Shepherdia canadensis) Red, oblong or round, sour-to-bitter fruit that Lewis thought "excellent" when he first found some on August 21, 1804, in future Nebraska.

currant (Ribes) Berries that ripen in late summer and range in taste from mild to sour to bitter. Often used in PEMMICAN. The Corps of Discovery ate and described several types; some were new to science.

huckleberry (Vaccinium globulare) Tart blueberry-like fruit of a Rocky Mountain shrub, a favorite of BEARS.

salmonberry (Rubus spectabilis Pursh) A fruit of the Lower Columbia that looks like a pinkish yellow raspberry, and has a very mild flavor. Indians mixed them with partly dried SALMON roe.

serviceberry (Amelanchier alnifolia) Saskatoon. This sweet, reddish-purple fruit is one of summer's first, ripening in June or early July. Often used in PEMMICAN. The captains also used the term for currants.

thimbleberry (Rubus parviflores) Relative of raspberry that is mushy and pale red when ripe.

serviceberry
COURTESY OF LARKSPUR BOOKS/ A. SCOTT EARLE

bearberry
COURTESY OF LARKSPUR BOOKS/A. SCOTT EARLE

buffalo berry
COURTESY OF LARKSPUR BOOKS/A. SCOTT EARLE

Biddle, Nicolas

Biddle, Nicholas (1786-1844) A PHILADELPHIA author and editor. When he worked with William Clark (and later, George SHANNON) beginning in 1810, Biddle wrote the first history of the expedition. He treated the journals as research notes, freely marking them with red ink. Two thousand copies of his *History of the Expedition Under the Command of Captains Lewis and Clark* were published in 1814. By agreement, this edition omitted Lewis's natural history notes, which were to be published separately and edited by Benjamin Smith BARTON.

Biddle is more famous as president of the second Bank of the United States, chartered by Congress for twenty years in 1816 to control the nation's currency. Appointed to its board of directors by President James Monroe, Biddle became bank president in 1823. Frontier and rural citizens saw the bank as biased in favor of eastern city residents, an issue that President Andrew Jackson seized upon. Biddle served as the human target of Jackson supporters' successful efforts not to recharter the bank in 1836.

Big Belly Indians Direct translation of GROS VENTRES, the French words for the Plains Indian sign language gesture that indicated both the HIDATSA Indians and the unrelated Atsina Indians.

Big Bend of the Missouri River In South Dakota, now covered by Lake Sharpe. When the Corps moved around it by water, they traveled 30 river miles. Across land, the distance was 1¼ miles, but their assignment was to measure the MISSOURI RIVER'S length, and they were taking the heavily loaded keelboat upstream.

bison (*Bos bison*) Often wrongly called buffalo. The Corps' hunters first saw them on June 28, 1804, near the Kansas River, but no one killed a bison until Joseph FIELD did on August 23, 1804, near the Nebraska–South Dakota border. Lewis took twelve men out to retrieve the beast. Bison were the men's favorite food, the tongue and hump being special treats. When the expedition entered the ROCKY MOUNTAINS in 1805, they left the bison behind until the following year. *See also* BOUDIN BLANC.

bitterroot *See* ROOT VEGETABLES.

bison
BOB EVERTON

Bitterroot Mountains Northern portion of the BITTERROOT RANGE of the ROCKY MOUNTAINS, extending roughly between Missoula, Montana, and Gibbonsville, Idaho. Crossing these mountains on the LOLO TRAIL, September 11-21, 1805, the Corps of Discovery entered the early stages of starvation. Game was so scarce in the already snow-covered mountains that they killed and ate some of the horses.

Bitterroot Range Part of the ROCKY MOUNTAINS that makes up most of the southeast-trending portion of the Montana-Idaho border. It includes the BITTERROOT and BEAVERHEAD mountains, both of which the Corps crossed.

Blackbird On August 11, 1804, the Corps of Discovery paused to pay their respects at Blackbird Hill in what is now Thurston County, Nebraska. Four hundred Omaha Indian people and their leader, Chief Blackbird, were buried there. They had died of smallpox, which the captains wrongly assumed had been passed to them by other Indians. In fact, it came from whites, with whom they had been friendly. The gravesite can be seen today from US 75 north of Decatur, Nebraska.

Black Buffalo Headman of the Teton SIOUX who met with the Corps near present Pierre, South Dakota, on September 25-28, 1804. He was friendlier to white traders than other Teton Sioux, and Clark noted that he was "said to be a good man."

Bitterroot Mountains
MONTANA MAGAZINE

Black Cat A chief of RUPTÁRE, whom the captains believed to be "Grand Chief of the Mandans." Just after the Corps' arrival among the MANDAN AND HIDATSA villages on October 28, 1804, Lewis and Clark and an interpreter walked out with Black Cat to find a timbered site for building their winter camp. To Lewis, writing on February 8, 1805, "this man possesses more integrety, firmness, inteligence and perpicuety…" than any other of their FORT MANDAN neighbors.

Blackfeet Indians BISON-hunting culture who ranged across future Montana and Alberta in 1806 when Lewis met them. The captains had been warned about the Blackfeet by other Indian nations who were their enemies, and Lewis did not expect a friendly welcome. He and his small Marias River exploration party met eight Piegan Blackfeet men on the Two Medicine River on July 26, 1806. (The site today is on the Blackfeet Indian Reservation, east of Glacier National Park in Montana.) They smoked together and Lewis believed he had given, through DROUILLARD'S sign language, the standard speech about the new government, and that it wanted Indian nations not to fight with each other and to welcome U.S. traders who would bring GUNS and other TRADE GOODS. The Blackfeet understood the message as a bald threat that the U.S. would unite and arm the Blackfeet's enemies. This led to the only Indian bloodshed committed by the Corps of Discovery. *See also* MARIAS RIVER.

Black Moccasin Head chief—to the captains—of METAHARTA. For a while this Hidatsa chief agreed to return to Washington, D.C., with them in 1806, then changed his mind. He was an old man when artist

Black Moccasin, by George Catlin
FROM THE COLLECTION OF GILCREASE MUSEUM, TULSA

George Catlin visited and did his portrait in 1833. Catlin wrote, in his book *Letters and Notes on the Manners, Customs, and Conditions of North American Indians*:

"The man has many distinct recollections of Lewis and Clarke [sic], who were the first explorers of this country, and who crossed the ROCKY MOUNTAINS thirty years ago."

It will be seen by reference to their very interesting history of their tour, that they were treated with great kindness by this man; and that they in consequence constituted him chief of the tribe, with the consent of his people; and he has remained their chief ever since. He enquired very earnestly for 'Red Hair' and 'Long Knife' (as he had ever since termed Lewis and Clarke), from the fact, that one [Clark] had red hair (an unexampled thing in his country), and the other wore a broad sword which gained for him the appellation of 'Long Knife.'

"I have told him that 'Long Knife' has been many years dead; and that 'Red Hair' is yet living in ST. LOUIS, and no doubt, would be glad to hear of him; at which he seemed much pleased, and has signified to me that he will make me bearer of some…dispatches to him."

bleeding An accepted medical practice of the time, bleeding meant drawing off blood (a cup or more), which doctors believed helped remove imagined infectious elements from the body (understanding of germs was a half-century in the future, in Louis Pasteur's work). Bleeding did no good at all, and weakened already sick people.

blubber Fat from sea mammals. On January 8, 1806, the Corps bought 300 pounds of whale blubber that Tillamook Indians harvested from a beached whale at today's Cannon Beach, Oregon. Clark said it cooked like pork fat but was spongier. Although they tried to make it last, the blubber was eaten up by January 29, 1806.

blunderbuss *See* GUNS.

boils Skin infection.

Boley, John (dates unknown) Private in the RETURN PARTY. In 1806, before the expedition returned home, he headed west again as part of the Zebulon Pike expedition that named Pikes Peak.

boudin blanc In French, "white pudding." A food of French voyageurs, this was CHARBONNEAU'S special contribution to the menu when the Corps was in BISON country. Using bison intestines as casing, Charbonneau stuffed them with bits of meat and the fat from the kidneys, mixed with salt and pepper and a little flour, boiled the result and then fried it in BEAR oil until brown. Everyone was very fond of this dish.

brace A pair, as in Lewis's braces of pistols (*see* GUNS), or a measurement of two arms' lengths, used for materials like ribbon, cloth, or BEADS.

brant (*Branta bernicla*) Small, mostly black goose about the size of a mallard duck. The captains often used the word, though, to refer to any type of goose, including the all-white snow goose (*Chen caerulescens*).

brant
BOB EVERTON

Bratton, William

Bratton, William (1778-1841) Private who enlisted with Clark at Clarksville, Indiana Territory, in 1803. He was in Sgt. ORDWAY'S squad, one of the blacksmiths, and one of three men nominated by the enlisted men to replace Sgt. Charles FLOYD. In 1806, he had a severe but mysterious back pain first mentioned on February 10, when he asked to return from SALT CAMP. The illness lasted until May 24, when John SHIELDS thought of building him a sauna; two weeks later, Lewis wrote that Bratton could no longer be considered an invalid.

breadroot *See* ROOT VEGETABLES.

buffalo *See* BISON.

buffalo berry *See* BERRIES.

bullboat Small, lightweight boat that MANDAN INDIANS and others made. BISON or other hides were attached to a bowl-shaped frame of willow. The Corps were impressed with how well they handled. Nathaniel PRYOR and others had occasion to make their own in 1806.

burning glass See SUN GLASS.

cache [*cash*] or **cached** A storage pit dug in the ground, or the act of making or using one. French voyageurs learned from Plains Indians to dig a hole, line it with animal hides and brush, then fill it with leather-wrapped items and cover it with dirt.

At the MARIAS RIVER on June 9, 1805, the Corps cached food, salt, gunpowder, lead, and some tools to pick up on the return trip. At the GREAT FALLS OF THE MISSOURI, they built caches at LOWER PORTAGE CAMP and UPPER PORTAGE CAMP, and cached some flour and salt, with plant and animal specimens. Unfortunately, spring flood water in 1806 soaked into one cache and destroyed all the specimens Lewis had collected between FORT MANDAN and the falls. The Corps also made large caches at CAMP FORTUNATE.

bullboat
FROM *THE TRAIL OF LEWIS AND CLARK*, BY OLIN D. WHEELER (1904)

Cahokia Courthouse In Cahokia, Illinois, this is one of the few man-made buildings still standing that Lewis and Clark visited. Lewis was often there during the winter of 1803-1804, Clark fewer times. Especially important to them was its service as post office, but it also was a gathering place for merchants and others who might have information about the country ahead. Today it is an Illinois State Historic Site.

Calumet Bluff The Corps of Discovery stayed at this site in future Nebraska from August 28 to September 1, 1804, to await the Yankton SIOUX and then meet in council with them. Named with the French word for the PEACE PIPE, Calumet Bluff is downstream on the MISSOURI RIVER from today's Gavins Point Dam.

camas See ROOT VEGETABLES.

Cameahwait, Chief Head of the Lemhi SHOSHONE INDIANS who helped the Corps cross the ROCKY MOUNTAINS, both by selling them horses and by carrying some of the baggage. Amazingly, he turned out to be SACAGAWEA'S brother. Tasting squash for the very first time (the captains had carried dried squash from the MANDAN AND HIDATSA villages), he told them that he would like peace so that his people could be safe and raise this delicious food.

camera obscura A box with a lens that projects a natural image into its interior, where it can be traced with pen or pencil. Lewis wished he had one on June 13, 1805, at the GREAT FALLS OF THE MISSOURI, being

Cahokia Courthouse
COURTESY CAHOKIA COURTHOUSE STATE HISTORIC SITE

Camp Chopunnish

frustrated with his ability to describe this surprising feature in words. Instead, he later sketched the falls freehand, but the drawings have been lost.

Camp Chopunnish Modern historians' term for a campsite the captains did not name (Chopunnish was the captains' mistaken name for the NEZ PERCE INDIANS). East of today's Nez Perce Indian Reservation and near Kamiah, Idaho, this is where the Corps stayed longest except for their winter encampments. Waiting for snow to melt in the mountains, they camped here in Nez Perce country from May 14 to June 10, 1806.

Camp Disappointment *See* MARIAS RIVER.

Camp Dubois, Camp Wood, or **Camp Wood River** Where the Corps of Discovery spent the winter before starting up the MISSOURI RIVER, from December 12, 1803, to May 14, 1804. Clark chose the site on the east (Illinois) side of the Mississippi River, across from ST. LOUIS. The Spanish governor of Upper Louisiana (administering for France), Carlos Dehault Delassus, told the Corps to stay on that side of the river, which was United States territory, because he had no official notice of the LOUISIANA PURCHASE yet.

The captains never gave the camp a name, and modern historians have used various ones. It was at the MOUTH of a river that had been named Rivière à Dubois for an early French resident, which was later mistranslated as Wood River.

Camp Fortunate What the captains called the campsite made after successfully meeting the SHOSHONE INDIANS. They stayed there August 17-24, 1805. Today

it is under the waters of Clark Canyon Reservoir, a lake formed at the headwaters of the JEFFERSON RIVER south of Dillon, Montana.

Camp White Catfish The Corps of Discovery took a working rest stop from July 22, 1804, to the 27th on the east (Iowa) side of the MISSOURI RIVER across from today's Bellevue, Nebraska. The camp was named for a fish that GOODRICH caught. Here the men made new oars and boat poles while the captains caught up on reports to send with the RETURN PARTY the next spring, and wrote out their speech for upcoming councils with Indians.

Camp Wood *See* CAMP DUBOIS.

Canoe Camp Camps where the expedition stopped to build CANOES for the next leg of their journey.

Sixteen men were sent out from FORT MANDAN late in February 1805 to locate a stand of timber and build canoes to carry freight that had been in the KEELBOAT the previous year. On March 9, 1805, Clark walked the five miles to their camp to check on progress. This canoe-building camp went unnamed in the journals.

The site that the captains actually named Canoe Camp was in use from September 26 to October 7, 1805, when those who were able built canoes for the downstream trek to the Pacific Ocean. Recovering from near-starvation while crossing the BITTERROOT RANGE, and getting used to a new diet of ROOT VEGETABLES and SALMON, most of the men were ill. Those who could work started digging out five large canoes, but not until October 3 did Clark write that everyone was able to help. On the CLEARWATER RIVER, five miles west of Orofino, Idaho, today the site is part of Nez Perce National Historical Park. The Corps also CACHED the pack saddles that had carried baggage across the mountains and would be used again the following spring.

On July 19, 1806, Clark's YELLOWSTONE RIVER party set up another unnamed canoe camp—south of today's Park City, Montana, where they stayed until July 24 making a pair of smaller canoes to lash together after George GIBSON'S injury.

canoes Sometimes refers to the PIROGUES as well as the smaller canoes. The Lewis and Clark Expedition's main means of travel from FORT MANDAN to the BEAVERHEAD RIVER, then down the COLUMBIA RIVER system to the Pacific in 1805, and back to ST. LOUIS in 1806. They built their own as needed (*see* CANOE CAMP), beginning with six made near FORT MANDAN between February 28 and March 20, 1805, to carry the baggage formerly in the KEELBOAT.

After the IRON BOAT failed, two canoes replacing it had to be built upstream from the GREAT FALLS OF THE MISSOURI. By August 7, the

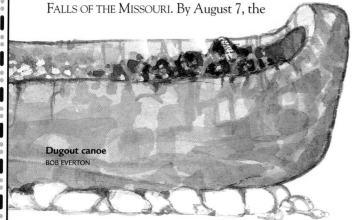

Dugout canoe
BOB EVERTON

Corps had used up enough supplies that one canoe could be CACHED in the vicinity of today's Twin Bridges, Montana. At CAMP FORTUNATE on August 23, Lewis cached the remaining canoes by sinking them, a way to hide them and also keep them safe from PRAIRIE fires.

Following the crossing of the ROCKY MOUNTAINS between the MISSOURI RIVER'S and the Columbia's highest waters, the captains set up Canoe Camp, where they had five canoes built for the remaining trip to the Pacific.

On the Columbia River, downstream from WISHRAM-WASCO INDIAN villages to the Pacific, the captains were impressed with the high-bowed local canoe design. Unlike the Corps' roughly shaped dugouts, it rode the ESTUARY'S waves well. The captains purchased one of these boats at CELILO FALLS on October 23, 1805. On November 11, 1805, while the Corps was stuck by waves too high for their canoes at Point Ellice, Washington, local Indians rowed up in their canoes to visit and sell some food. On the 13th, COLTER, SHANNON, and

Columbia River dugout canoe at Celilo Falls, 1897
REPRODUCED FROM THE COLLECTIONS OF THE LIBRARY OF CONGRESS

Cape Disappointment

WILLARD become the first expedition members to reach the Pacific Ocean when they were sent downstream in the recently-purchased Columbia canoe.

During the winter at FORT CLATSOP, with the tidal effects of the Columbia ESTUARY on the NETUL RIVER and other creeks, the precious boats sometimes floated away at night, and men were sent to hunt them. The Columbia Indian canoe was lost from January 11 to February 5, 1806.

On the YELLOWSTONE RIVER in 1806, Clark planned to make canoes when he found large enough trees. But after GIBSON suffered a bad wound on July 18, Clark stopped the next day to set up a CANOE CAMP and build two boats that were lashed together for stability. This dual canoe was used on down the MISSOURI RIVER until being set adrift near the Gasconade River in future Missouri on September 20.

After Clark's YELLOWSTONE RIVER party and Lewis's MARIAS RIVER party reunited in August 1806, all stopped to visit the MANDAN AND HIDATSA INDIANS, say farewell to the CHARBONNEAU family, and pick up new passengers. Chief SHEHEKE and his family, with interpreter René JUSSEAUME and his family, were traveling to Washington, D.C. To give the women and children a stable ride, Clark ordered the two largest canoes tied together with poles.

Cape Disappointment Although the Corps of Discovery were miserable here, they did not bestow the name. British captain John Meares had named this hook of land between the COLUMBIA RIVER'S Baker Bay and the Pacific Ocean, south of present Ilwaco, Washington, in 1788. His disappointment was failure to find the MOUTH of the Columbia, approaching from the Pacific. When Robert GRAY located the Columbia four years later, he named the point of land "Cape Hancock." But the more colorful name stuck.

capote (pronounced *cuh*-POAT) Simple hooded coat made by voyageurs and indians from woolen blankets or animal hides.

capote
BOB EVERTON

high-bowed Columbia River canoe
BOB EVERTON

Carolina parakeet (*Conuropsis carolinensis*) When Clark wrote on June 26, 1804, that they had seen a great number of "Parrot queets," it was the first scientific notice of the Carolina parakeet west of the Mississippi. This species, which the Corps saw near the MOUTH of the Kansas River, went extinct in the 1920s, killed off by farmers.

Carolina parakeet
BOB EVERTON

Cascades of the Columbia Now under the waters of Bonneville DAM just south of Bridge of the Gods near Stevenson, Washington, and Cascade Locks, Oregon.

The Corps of Discovery PORTAGED a mile and a half around the Cascades on November 2, 1805, and en route home on April 12, 1806.

Celilo Falls To the captains, the "Great Falls of the Columbia River," then just upstream from THE DALLES and today under water raised by The Dalles DAM. The falls were downstream from the MOUTH of the Deschutes River (in Oregon) at present Wishram, Washington. The Corps arrived on October 22, 1805, finding fifty-eight Indian lodges in the area, which was a regional trading site. Locals told the captains their pounded SALMON was traded to whites on the seacoast.

The next day, some of the Corps walked a 1,200-foot PORTAGE around Celilo Falls on the Washington side, aided by local Indians with horses. Clark and most of the men crossed to today's Oregon (south) side and used towropes to let the canoes down the falls; one got loose but Indians caught it.

Celilo Falls was reached on the return trip on April 21, 1806. With Clark going ahead and purchasing horses to carry baggage, Lewis was able to trade two canoes for beads here. Because Indians were taking things and seemed to have let loose the horses, Lewis angrily burned a third canoe.

Celilo Falls
FROM *THE TRAIL OF LEWIS AND CLARK*, BY OLIN D. WHEELER (1904)

Celilo Falls and THE DALLES marked the border between languages of the Shahaptian family that included Nez Perce, and the Chinookan family that extended to the Pacific coast. The area was a major trading point before the Corps visited it.

Charbonneau, Jean Baptiste (1805-1866) The son of SACAGAWEA and Toussaint CHARBONNEAU, born February 11, 1805, was fifty-five days old when the Corps of Discovery and his family left the MANDAN AND HIDATSA villages for the Pacific Ocean. Along the way, he teethed, suffered miserably from mosquito bites at times, took his first steps, and said his first words. Captain Clark was especially fond of him, and offered to raise and educate the boy at his St. Louis home. Clark nicknamed the boy "Pompy," and named POMPEYS PILLAR for him. Around 1811, the Charbonneaus took Clark up on his offer, and Jean Baptiste lived with Clark's family until he was eighteen years old.

Charbonneau, Toussaint (ca. 1758–ca. 1839-1843) Hired as a translator because he had two SHOSHONE wives, and was to take one along from FORT MANDAN to the Pacific. The one who went was SACAGAWEA. Charbonneau spoke little English, so one of the French speakers translated to him for the captains. He had lived among the Hidatsas for many years and spoke that language, but not the Shoshone that was his wife's native tongue, so he spoke to her in Hidatsa. He was a fearful boatman, generally not a useful hand, but the men enjoyed his cooking—*see also* BOUDIN BLANC.

After the expedition, he and Sacagawea had a second child, who was christened Lisette. While Clark was Superintendent of Indian Affairs for upper LOUISIANA, he sometimes hired Charbonneau as a translator. He was living in the MANDAIDATSA villages when Duke Maximillian of Weid-Neuweid visited in 1833, and translated for the German prince and his party.

Che-luc-it-te-quar *See* WISHRAM-WASCO INDIANS.

Chien Indians During 1804, Clark wrote several times about the "Dog" Indians. The captains had misunderstood references to the Cheyenne Indians (whom they never met) as being named with the French word for dog, "chien," until someone at FORT MANDAN corrected them.

Chimnapam One of the captains' names for Yakama Indians.

chokecherry Small, very tart cherries that ripen in August. They were dried, pounded, and added to stews or PEMMICAN.

Chopunnish The captains' name for NEZ PERCE INDIANS.

chokecherry
LARKSPUR BOOKS/A. SCOTT EARLE

chronometer An extremely accurate time-piece designed to survive motion, moisture, and changes in climate. Knowing the exact time was essential to figuring LONGITUDE for mapmaking. The chronometer Lewis purchased in Philadelphia cost $250.75 ($2,786.11 in present dollars), which was 60% of the cost of all his navigation instruments.

Chymnappos One of the captains' names for Yakama Indians.

circumferentor Surveyor's compass with sights opposite each other and a compass between, held level on a pole or tripod. The captains' measured 6" across.

circumferentor
BOB EVERTON

The user looked from one sight through the other at a fixed object in the distance, then used the compass to read the bearing (AZIMUTH) or relative position of the object and the observer. Clark did this constantly for his COURSES, notes that he later used for mapping. He also took "back" readings: when he reached the fixed object, he would look back to his last position and take the bearing from the object to where he had been. At the time, bearings were written in degrees of each quarter of the compass, so might read N 82° E for an object ahead on the right.

This item was so essential that when a flash flood tore it away from Clark on June 29, 1805, at the Great Falls of the Missouri, he took two men off PORTAGE detail and sent them to comb the river's edge for it the next day. They found it after digging into mud, sand, and rocks the flood had deposited.

Clark's circumferentor made it safely home with him, and today is owned by the National Museum of American History, Smithsonian Institution, Washington, D.C.

Clark, George Rogers (1752-1818) William's older brother, a Revolutionary War general who won the western frontier (Ohio and Indiana) from the British.

Clark, William (1770-1838) When Clark was fourteen, his family moved from Virginia to the Kentucky frontier. Beginning in 1792, he served in the U.S. Army during the Northwest campaign against Indians allied with the British. By the time he left the army, he was a captain, and had been Meriwether Lewis's commanding officer. Lewis invited him to join the expedition as co-captain, but Secretary of War Henry Dearborn required that Clark's rank be lieutenant.

Clark was an experienced surveyor who learned from Lewis the techniques of celestial navigation, and made most of the COURSES' observations. He drew maps in the field and during the FORT MANDAN and FORT CLATSOP winters.

After the expedition, Clark served as superintendent of Indian affairs for nations west of the Mississippi River, in addition to political offices that included being the last governor of Missouri Territory.

William Clark, by Charles Willson Peale
COURTESY INDEPENDENCE NATIONAL PARK, PHILADELPHIA

Clark Fork River and **Clarks Fork Yellowstone River** *Clark Fork River* forms near the CONTINENTAL DIVIDE in Montana, between Anaconda and Butte, flowing north-northwest through Missoula, Montana, into Lake Pend Oreille in Idaho. When the Corps was westward-bound in 1805, the Clark Fork River was

Confluence of the Clarks Fork Yellowstone with the Yellowstone River LARRY MAYER

the "FLATHEAD River" to the captains, but on May 6, 1806, Lewis renamed it in Clark's honor.

Clarks Fork Yellowstone River flows out of the Beartooth Mountains in Montana, through Wyoming east of Yellowstone National Park, then back into Montana to its MOUTH on the YELLOWSTONE RIVER at the town of Laurel. On July 24, 1806, Clark's party came to the mouth of a river that the captain first took to be the Bighorn River, which Indians had described. Two days later, they reached the Bighorn itself, and Clark changed the name of the earlier river to Clark's Fork of the Yellowstone, which today is written without the apostrophe or "of the."

Clark's nutcracker *See* JAY.

Clatsop Indians The Corps of Discovery moved into the Clatsops' neighborhood along today's Lewis and Clark River south of Astoria, Oregon, to spend the winter of 1805-1806. They were not as close friends as the MANDAN INDIANS had been the previous winter, and the captains found aspects of their culture less appealing. A small tribe then (the captains estimated 300 members), the Clatsops dipped to twenty-six people living on Grande Ronde Reservation in 1910. The reservation was terminated in 1956, but Clatsops are now again recognized by the U.S. government.

Clearwater River The first major stream of the COLUMBIA RIVER system that the Corps followed downstream in future Idaho to its MOUTH on the SNAKE RIVER at today's Lewiston, Idaho, and Clarkston, Washington. The captains called it the Kooskee, or Kooskooskee, River. Clark and an advance party first reached it on September 22, 1805, and the whole party traveled it October 8–10, 1805.

clothing, Army issue *Enlisted men* were issued two cloth shirts, one wool waistcoat, one leather neck stock (necktie; it was leather as protection against sword wounds), one pair of navy wool overalls for winter and

linen shirt
J. AGEE

Enlisted man's coat and "round hat" from 1803 J. AGEE PHOTOS

one pair of white wool for summer, one pair of white linen fatigue overalls, one dress coat, one dress hat, one white linen rifle shirt, one hooded and belted coat, one pair of low leather shoes, and two pairs of socks. The shirt's long tails were tucked into the breeches, serving in place of underpants.

Members of the Corps who enlisted in the Army especially for the expedition, including the nine young men from KENTUCKY, were issued buff-colored coats (which Lewis had had made in Pittsburgh).

Officers' coats and hats had more and finer decoration, and their dress uniforms included swords. *See also* ESPONTOON.

Officers and enlisted men wore dress uniforms for the formal councils with Indians, for COURTS MARTIAL, and possibly for Charles FLOYD'S funeral. When TRADE GOODS were running low in the early months of 1806, the captains cut the brass buttons off their uniforms to trade for food; later, the enlisted men used the pewter ones from theirs.

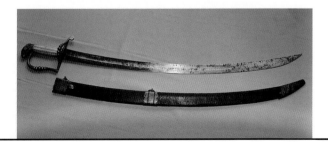

Officer's Napoleon-style hat (above), coat, and sword with sheath (left) J. AGEE PHOTOS

clothing, leather From the middle of May to the end of July, 1805, the men's summer army fatigue clothing wore out and they began TANNING hides (usually ELK) and stitching simple garments. These too wore out quickly because the leather was almost always wet. During the FORT CLATSOP winter, the men stockpiled new leather clothing, so that on February 23, 1806, Lewis wrote that they now had more clothing and MOCCASINS than they had since starting out. *See also* TIPPET.

Coboway, Chief A neighbor of FORT CLATSOP who was the friendliest to the Corps during the winter of 1805-1806. Upon leaving, they gave the fort to him and he lived there for some years.

colic To the captains, any intestinal illness.

Collins, John (?-1823) Private in Sgt. PRYOR'S squad. Possibly transferred to the expedition from the army infantry. He was COURT MARTIALLED at St. Charles, Missouri, on May 17, 1804, for being AWOL, "unbecomming" behavior at a civilian dance, and speaking disrespectfully to Clark upon returning to camp. The sentence was fifty lashes of the whip, carried out that same day. On the night of June 28-29 the same year, at the site of future Kansas City, Kansas, Collins was on guard duty when he allowed Hugh HALL to break into the whiskey supply and joined in drinking it. While HALL was sentenced to fifty lashes, Collins received 100 lashes for both allowing the theft and then taking advantage of it.

Colter, John (ca. 1775-1813) Private in Sgt. ORDWAY'S squad, who probably enlisted with Lewis on the OHIO RIVER in 1803. One of the most valued members of the expedition as hunter and tracker, he didn't return home in 1806, but requested an early discharge from the army to return to the Upper Missouri with trappers the Corps met in future North Dakota. He was the first white to report on the wonders that today are in Yellowstone National Park, which disbelieving mountain men jokingly nicknamed "Colter's Hell." *See also* CANOES.

Columbia River The captains knew of this river from the writings of George VANCOUVER. The Corps traveled downstream on it beginning October 16, 1805. With the main group stopped by bad weather and high waves in the Columbia ESTUARY, November 10-15, the captains sent COLTER, SHANNON, and WILLARD ahead to the Pacific coast. They thus became the Corps' first members to travel the entire Columbia when they reached its MOUTH on November 13. *See also* CASCADES OF THE COLUMBIA, CELILO FALLS, DAMS, GREAT CHUTE, THE DALLES.

Columbia River Gorge The Columbia River flows through this eighty-mile-long canyon at sea level, cutting as much as 4,000' down through the Cascade Mountains, which rise to 1,300'-1,500' in the area. The gorge begins from east of Wishram, Washington, across from the MOUTH of the Deschutes River in Oregon. It extends downstream to east of Washougal on the Washington side, and the mouth of the Sandy River on the Oregon side.

The Corps passed the mouth of the Deschutes River on October 22, 1805, and reached the Sandy River on November 3. They had PORTAGED and/or run CELILO FALLS, THE DALLES, the GREAT CHUTE, and the

CASCADES OF THE COLUMBIA in the interim. (Bonneville DAM has raised the river's waters above all these obstacles.) After their hard days' work, the men often danced to fiddle music at night, sometimes to the amusement of various Indian nations gathered here for the autumn SALMON run.

In 1986, the gorge was designated the 292,500-acre Columbia River Gorge National Scenic Area, to encourage economic uses compatible with scenic values.

compass In PHILADELPHIA in 1803, Lewis purchased a silver-plated pocket compass and three brass pocket compasses, along with one brass boat compass and a surveyor's compass (*see* CIRCUMFERENTOR).

Clark carried his personal compass, which had a wooden case and fitted into a leather pouch. It was about the size of a man's palm, and could be carried in a large pocket. Like his circumferentor, today it is owned by the National Museum of American History, Smithsonian Institution, Washington, D.C.

compass
BOB EVERTON ILLUSTRATIONS

condor, California (*Gymnogyps californianus*) Vulture that is 45" to 55" long with a wingspan up to 9.5'. It was not new to science when SHANNON and LABICHE delivered a wounded one to the captains at FORT CLATSOP on February 16,

California condor
BOB EVERTON

1806. Lewis thought it the largest North American bird. He was correct; the birds are the largest living bird species. Nearly extinct in the wild in North America until restoration attempts began in the 1980s, condors also live in the Andes of South America. In the spring of 2002, in California and for the first time in the U.S. for eighteen years, a condor chick hatched in the wild.

Continental Divide The natural dividing line in North America between where water flows toward the Atlantic Ocean or toward the Pacific Ocean.

cooking utensils Six brass kettles, a sauce pan, and a corn mill that fascinated Indians who ground CORN with stones, made up the kitchen outfit. Meat was roasted or boiled over the open fire, and also JERKED. By the time the expedition was homeward bound in the spring of 1806, the Corps were down to only one kettle, having given or traded the others away.

cordelle When the MISSOURI RIVER was shallow and there was a flat bank to walk on, the men had to attach ropes to the boats, especially the KEELBOAT, and tow them upstream. This method was also used to lift boats over rapids and rocky areas of the streambed. After their ropes wore out, the men made new ones by laboriously twisting strips of ELK hide into tight cords.

cordelling
ROBERT F. MORGAN

corn Maize. To preserve corn for storage, it is parched by baking the moisture out of the kernels. The Corps started out with five barrels of parched corn. Hominy, or lyed corn, is whole or coarsely ground field corn soaked in lye water then rinsed to remove the hull (bran). It also can be parched. The Corps' supply was twenty-five and a half bushels.

Coues, Elliott (1842-1899) Ornithologist hired to produce a revised edition of Nicholas BIDDLE'S *History of the Expedition Under the Command of Captains Lewis and Clark*, which was published in 1893. He organized all the journals and loose papers by date, and added some of Lewis's natural history information and more quotations from the journals to Biddle's text. He also treated the journals roughly, thoroughly marking them up; historian Gary MOULTON states that Coues "shamelessly defaced" these historic artefacts.

Council Bluff The Corps camped from July 30 to August 3, 1804, at the future site of Fort Calhoun, Nebraska, where they named "The Council Bluff." Since then, the Missouri River has shifted eastward away from their bluff. The city of Council Bluffs, Iowa, later developed to the south and across the Missouri.

courses The journals include "COURSES and distances" giving the daily COMPASS bearings of landmarks along the path traveled. These were figured with relatively simple instruments: CHRONOMETER, CIRCUMFERENTOR, SEXTANT, OCTANT, and books of charts. Besides tracing the MISSOURI RIVER to its source, the captains were assigned to map it. Clark was an experienced surveyor, and Lewis received a crash course in celestial navigation from Robert PATTERSON and Andrew ELLICOTT in 1803, then passed the knowledge on to Clark. Clark drew most of the maps working from his "daily courses" notes both in the field and during the winters at FORT MANDAN and FORT CLATSOP. *See also* LATITUDE, LONGITUDE.

court martial Trial held by the military for a soldier accused of disobeying orders or breaking rules or regulations. Lewis and Clark held them on six occasions, the last on February 10, 1805. *See also* John COLLINS, Hugh HALL, Thomas HOWARD, John NEWMAN, Moses REED, William WERNER, Alexander WILLARD.

cous or **cows** *See* ROOT VEGETABLES.

coyote *(Canis latrans)* To the captains, the small "prairie wolf's" yipping bark sounded like that of domesticated dogs. They first saw coyotes on August 12, 1804, in future Iowa, but Lewis described the species in detail on May 5, 1805, in today's McCone County, Montana. He referred to it as a small wolf or burrowing dog that had piercing, deep sea-green eyes.

coyote
DONALD M. JONES

cradleboard A board with attached leather pouch, decorated with quillwork or beadwork, for a mother to carry her baby on her back. Although SACAGAWEA is often portrayed as carrying her son on a cradleboard, as her SHOSHONE people did, Lewis and Clark scholar Joseph A. Mussulman argues that she would have followed the HIDATSA style. She had lived with the Hidatsas for five years by the time she became a mother. Hidatsa women put a large shawl-like wrapping around the baby and the mother's shoulders.

On the Lower Columbia, some Indian nations used a top piece on cradleboards to flatten and shape the baby's forehead. This mark of beauty was allowed only to people of higher status, and in some tribes limited to girls. The SALISH INDIANS that the captains misnamed "Flatheads" did not follow this procedure.

Cruzatte, Pierre (dates unknown) Private in Sgt. PRYOR'S squad. He officially enlisted at St. Charles, Missouri, two days after the expedition's start. His father was French and his mother Omaha, so he translated those languages. He was also the Corps' main fiddler. He had been as far up the Missouri as the MANDAN villages, and was the Corps' most experienced

ROBERT F. MORGAN

river PILOT. Before the expedition, he had lost an eye, which may have contributed to his accidentally shooting Meriwether Lewis on August 11, 1806, when both were hunting ELK in the brush—wearing elk skin clothing.

currant *See* BERRIES.

Dame, John (1784-?) Private in RETURN PARTY. Transferred to the expedition from the army artillery.

dams Since the Lewis and Clark Expedition traveled, dams have created lakes or deep water that cover the former channels and often the riverbank campsites the Corps made. They also make it impossible for anyone to canoe the entire route now exactly as the Corps did.

On the OHIO RIVER, going downstream, the dams are: Emsworth (1921), Dashields (1929), Montgomery (1936), New Cumberland (1959), Pike Island (1963), Hannibal (1972), Willow Island (1972), Belleville (1965), Racine (1967), Robert C. Byrd (1937), Greenup (1962), Meldahl (1964), Markland (1963), McAlpine (1961), Cannelton (1972), Newburgh (1975), Uniontown (1975), Smithland (1980), Lock and Dam 52 (1928), Lock and Dam 53 (1929).

On the MISSOURI RIVER, going upstream, dams (and the lakes that some form) are Gavins Point Dam, 1957 (Lewis and Clark Lake), Fort Randall Dam, 1954 (Lake Francis Case), Big Bend Dam, 1966 (Lake Sharpe), Oahe Dam, 1962 (Lake Oahe), Garrison Dam, 1956 (Lake Sakakawea), Fort Peck Dam, 1940 (Fort Peck Lake), Ryan Dam, 1915, Rainbow Dam, 1910, Black Eagle Dam, 1891, Holter Dam, 1918 (Holter Lake), Hauser Dam, 1911 (Hauser Lake), Canyon Ferry Dam, 1954 (Canyon Ferry Lake).

On the SNAKE RIVER, going downstream, they are: Lower Granite Dam, 1978 (Lower Granite Lake), Lower Monumental Dam, 1969 (Lake Herbert G. West), Ice Harbor Dam, 1961 (Lake Sacajawea).

On the COLUMBIA RIVER, going downstream, they are: McNary Dam, 1953 (Lake Wallula), John Day Dam, 1971 (Lake Umatilla), The Dalles Dam, 1957 (Lake Celilo). In the COLUMBIA RIVER GORGE, Bonneville Dam (1937) raises the Columbia's waters over the GREAT CHUTE and CASCADES OF THE COLUMBIA.

deer Everyone in the Corps of Discovery was familiar with the white-tailed deer (*Odocoileus virginianus*), because it lived throughout the East then as it does today. Lewis referred to it as the "common deer."
mule deer (*Odocoileus hemionus*) was new to science when Lewis and Clark first described it. They gave it the name that has stayed, because its ears are much larger than those of the white-tailed deer.
Columbia black-tailed deer (*Odocoileus hemionus*) is

mule deer
DONALD M. JONES

now thought to be the same species as the mule deer, but it is smaller, and lives only in the humid woods in the Pacific Northwest.

Deschamps, Jean Baptiste (dates unknown) The "patroon," or boss, of the hired French boatmen who accompanied the Corps to the MANDAN villages, where they were paid and discharged.

dinner The largest meal of the day, eaten at mid-day. In the evening, the Corps "supped."

dinosaurs Scientists of the day thought that perhaps prehistoric animals still roamed the middle of the continent, so Lewis was ordered to report on them. The Corps saw some fossils, and traveled unknowingly through or near some of North America's best fossil country in the Dakotas and Montana.

Dog Indians *See* CHIEN INDIANS.

dogwood, red osier (*Cornus sericea*) Shrub of wet areas on the plains and in the mountains. Indians mixed the roots' inner bark into their ceremonial smoking mixture, and men of the Corps used it also, on the return trip before they reached the CACHED tobacco at CAMP FORTUNATE.

dragoon A large flintlock handgun. *See* GUNS: *pistols.*

dram Scottish term for a small drink. A fluid *drachm* is one eighth of an ounce, but when the captains wrote, "We gave the men a dram [of whiskey]," they were not being literal.

Drewyer The captains' constant phonetic misspelling of DROUILLARD.

Drouillard, George (?-1810) A hired civilian, he was the most valuable man of the expedition after the captains. His father was French, his mother Shawnee, and he probably was already working for the U.S. Army as a translator. Besides speaking English and his parents' languages, he knew Plains Indian sign. He joined the expedition at FORT MASSAC in 1803 upon meeting Lewis, but did not enlist in the army. He returned to the ROCKY MOUNTAINS as a fur trader after the expedition, and was killed by BLACKFEET INDIANS near the MISSOURI RIVER'S HEADWATERS in 1810.

E-chee-lutes or **Echelutes** *See* WISHRAM-WASCO INDIANS.

eagle On July 11, 1805, Lewis compared golden eagles (new to him) and bald eagles, which he had seen flying, and drew a mistaken conclusion. He believed that western bald eagles were smaller than those familiar in the east, and also that the golden eagle was larger. Today's scientists think he may have compared a female bald eagle to a male golden.

bald (*Haliaeetus leucocephalus*) The American national emblem can be 30" to 43" long, dark brown with a white head and tail. It eats mostly dead or dying fish. At the time, it still lived in many parts of the U.S., but on April 14, 1805, in future North Dakota, Lewis wrote that they were seeing a greater concentration of bald eagles than ever. Their population today is concentrated in the southern Cascade Range, the northern Rockies, and along

espontoon
BOB EVERTON

the Pacific coast from Oregon to Alaska.

golden (Aquila chrysaetos) Ranging from 30" to 40", the bird is dark brown all over, with a touch of gold on the back of the head. It lives on rabbits and large rodents. This eagle's feathers often adorned Indian smoking pipes, and Lewis learned from an ARIKARA chief to call it the "calumet" (PEACE PIPE) bird. Golden eagles live from the northern edges of British Columbia, Alberta, and western Saskatchewan through the American West into western Mexico.

elk *(Cervus elaphus canadensis)* The main source of food for the Corps when they were not in BISON country, and also the source of leather for clothing. It was nearly the only red meat eaten during the entire FORT CLATSOP stay. They also were hunted on the Great Plains. A large member of the DEER family, the elk is 4'-5' tall and males weigh up 1,000 pounds. Males also have a mane. Today they live in the ROCKY MOUNTAINS and along the northern Pacific Coast of the U.S.

Ellicott, Andrew (1754-1820) This astronomer/ mathematician, official Surveyor of the United States, welcomed Lewis into his Lancaster, Pennsylvania, home from April 20 to May 10, 1803. A former student of Robert PATTERSON, he taught the captain navigation and astronomical observation for the

Ellicott's home, where Lewis studied BARBARA FIFER

mapmaking part of his duties. Ellicott also wrote the shopping list of navigation instruments that Lewis would purchase, and developed an improved ARTIFICIAL HORIZON for the captains' use in rough terrain.

espontoon Beginning to go out of use at the time, this was a long spear-like item also called a half-pike. They served to identify infantry officers on the battlefield, and for signalling. At about six feet, it was as long as Lewis was tall. He used it as a walking staff, and sometimes to steady the long barrel of his heavy rifle for shooting. On July 14, 1805, at the GREAT FALLS OF THE MISSOURI, Lewis even faced a charging grizzly BEAR with only his espontoon and an empty GUN. Happily, the bear called off its attack.

estuary The MOUTH of a large river on an ocean, where salt water and fresh water mix, tidal effects occur, and waves develop. On November 7, 1805, the Corps of Discovery reached the upper end of the COLUMBIA RIVER estuary and camped on the Washington side opposite PILLAR ROCK. Clark wrote: "Great joy in camp we are in *View* of the *Ocian*, this great Pacific Octean which we been So long anxious to See." It would be six more days until the first men reached the Pacific itself.

evening In general usage then, and lingering in the southern states into the 20th century, the word meant the time from noon to twilight or the evening meal. The captains often write about 3 p.m. as being "at 3 in the evening."

eyewash or **eye water** Eye drops of lead acetate and zinc sulfate that the captains used to soothe the expedition's and Indians' eyes suffering from snow glare, blowing sand, or infections.

fathom Linear measurement of 6 feet, usually used for water depth now, but Clark often used it to refer to distance on land.

Field, Joseph (1772-1807) and **Reubin** (1771-1823?) Privates who enlisted with Clark in 1803. The captains always misspelled the last name as Fields. They were in Sgt. FLOYD'S squad, and were brothers. Both were very good hunters and reliable men who were often chosen for small separated parties, such as Lewis's return exploration of the MARIAS RIVER.

fire steel The two-piece item that served the Corps as matches. A C-shaped piece of high-carbon steel is clamped in the fingers of one hand, while a piece of flint (the same the men used in their GUNS) is struck on it to make sparks. These were popular TRADE GOODS.

Flathead Indians The captains' name for the SALISH INDIANS. *See also* CRADLEBOARD.

flintlock See GUNS: *rifle*.

Floyd, Charles (1782-1804) Sergeant who enlisted with Clark at Clarksville, Indiana Territory, in 1803. He was Nathaniel PRYOR'S cousin. The only man who didn't survive the expedition, he died on August 19, 1804, near the future site of Sergeant Bluff, Iowa, probably from infection caused by a ruptured appendix. The

Corps gave him a military funeral at the place they named "Floyd's Bluff," today's Sergeant Bluff. By 1857, the moving MISSOURI RIVER had eaten away at the bluff, and Floyd's remains were moved to Sioux City, Iowa. In 1901 he was reburied yet again, and a tall monument erected at the grave. At that time, a cast was made of his skull; from it a collateral descendent recreated Floyd's image using forensic science.

Fort Bellefontaine Built on the Missouri River west of ST. LOUIS in 1805, it was the first U.S. Army post west of the Mississippi. In 1806, the Corps of Discovery stopped to see the new fort built in their absence, and outfitted their Indian guests with clothing from the public store.

The recreated, life-size Floyd image is at Sioux City Lewis & Clark Interpretive Center, Sioux City, Iowa
COURTESY OF SIOUX CITY PUBLIC MUSEUM

Fort Clatsop

Fort Clatsop The rough shelter the men built for themselves and the CHARBONNEAU family to spend the winter of 1805-1806 near the Pacific coast (at today's Astoria, Oregon). Because Clark drew a sketch in his journal, the National Park Service has been able to reconstruct Fort Clatsop.

Winter here was trying for all the men, woman, baby, and dog. Food was scarce, maddening fleas plentiful, rain and cloudy skies constant (on only twelve days was there no rain, and on only six was there sun), and the Americans had met their trek's objectives and were ready to head for home.

When the expedition left for home in March 1806, they gave the "fort" to Chief COBOWAY of the CLATSOP INDIANS, because he had been "much more kind and hospitable to us" than any other neighbor that winter. Coboway lived in it for some time and, in 1899, his grandson showed a historian where the fort's remains had stood when he was a boy.

Fort Kaskaskia At Ellis Grove, Illinois, across the Mississippi River from Ste. Genevieve, Missouri. Reaching this fort in the ILLINOIS on November 27, 1803, the captains split up for the first of many times. Lewis stayed at Fort Kaskaskia until December 5. He put Clark in charge of the boats, which left for CAHOKIA on December 3. Lewis went with two local French/English-speakers to ST. LOUIS to inform the fort's French and Spanish-speaking commandant about the LOUISIANA PURCHASE.

Fort Clatsop National Memorial, Astoria, Oregon J. AGEE

Fort Mandan The Corps of Discovery arrived at the MANDAN AND HIDATSA villages in future northwestern North Dakota on October 26, 1804, and left on April 7, 1805. Construction of their "fort" started on November 2. They spent quite a congenial winter here, because these farming villages traded their produce to other Indians and to white fur traders from Canada.

Fort Mandan
ROBERT F. MORGAN

Visitors arrived regularly, breaking up the monotony of long winter nights. Men of the Corps joined the neighbors in hunting trips. The captains quizzed everyone they could—whites and Indians—about what to expect upstream on the MISSOURI RIVER, and received very helpful information. Clark drew maps of 1804's travel, and both captains prepared writings and specimens to send with the RETURN PARTY in spring 1805.

Fort Massac At today's Metropolis, Illinois, on the OHIO RIVER. The French built the first fort here in 1757 and rebuilt it by 1760. After the French and Indian War ended in 1763, French soldiers abandoned the fort. English troops sent to garrison it found it burned down by Chickasaw Indians, and did not rebuild. Its absence helped George Rogers CLARK take Illinois Territory from the British in 1778, during the Revolutionary War. Lewis, Clark, and some of the men stopped here on November 11-13, 1803. They made their best, and one of their worst, selections of men here, hiring George DROUILLARD and adding John NEWMAN. Fort Massac State Park includes a reconstruction of the fort.

Fort Rock campsite Locally known as Rock Fort. At the townsite of today's The Dalles, Oregon, the Corps camped here October 25-28, 1805, to rest and dry freight after navigating THE DALLES.

On the return trip, the corps stayed here from April 15 to 18, 1806, hunting and trading for horses.

Fort Rock campsite
FROM *THE TRAIL OF LEWIS AND CLARK*, BY OLIN D. WHEELER (1904)

fox, swift (*Vulpes velox*) Smaller than the red fox, and with coloration like the COYOTE, the species was new to science when Lewis first noted (July 6, 1805) seeing small foxes that live in burrows like coyotes. Two days later, still near the GREAT FALLS OF THE MISSOURI, one of the men brought Lewis a specimen and he wrote in detail about its characteristics. This female was smaller than a house cat, he said. The swift fox grows 15"-20" long, with a 9"-12" tail, and weighing 4-6 pounds.

Frazer, Robert (?-1837) Private in Sgt. FLOYD'S squad. Whether he already was in the army is unknown. Was to have been in the RETURN PARTY, but the captains transferred him to the PERMANENT PARTY after Moses REED'S desertion. He voluntarily kept a journal that has been lost. The book to be based on it was announced for publication with Lewis's blessing, but never came out.

frostbite Exposure to severe low temperatures causes water in the skin to freeze, cutting off the area's blood supply. This was a constant danger during the winter at FORT MANDAN, and several of the men suffered some degree of frostbite. Even in the milder winter at CAMP DUBOIS, Clark had written on January 9, 1804, that his feet froze to his shoes when he walked out to hunt and visit Cahokia Mounds. He used the standard medical treatment of the day, putting his feet into cold water—just the opposite of what was useful.

During the Fort Mandan winter, the journals mention that men of the Corps "fre-quently, were slightly frosted" when they went out to hunt. From December 7, 1804, through February 16, 1805, seven occasions were bad enough for specific mention. Named victims were YORK, WHITEHOUSE, Joseph FIELD, and HOWARD.

The worse case of frostbite the men saw on the trip, however, was that of a thirteen-year-old MANDAN boy who was lost from a hunting party and spent the night of January 9-10, 1805, out on the prairie without fire, a tent, or heavy clothing. The captains used the cold-water treatment at once. But the injury was severe, and Lewis amputated some of the boy's toes on January 27 and more of them on the 31st.

No cases occurred in the mild climate of FORT CLATSOP.

Gallatin River *See* THREE FORKS OF THE MISSOURI RIVER.

Patrick Gass

Gass, Patrick (1771-1870) Sergeant; earlier, a private in Sgt. FLOYD'S squad. Transferred to the expedition from the army infantry. After Floyd's death, the men nominated him as sergeant and the captains promoted him on August 26, 1804. His carpentry skills were put to use building the three sets of winter quarters. Gass published his own expedition journal, rewritten by a professional, in 1807—the first in print. The book had no approval from Lewis, who condemned it along with other "spurious" accounts that might be written by non-participants. Gass was the expedition's last survivor.

Gates of the Rocky Mountains What Lewis named a narrow, six-mile-long canyon on the Missouri River near present Helena, Montana. Today it is known as Gates of the Mountains.

Gates of the Mountains
MONTANA MAGAZINE

Gibson, George (?-1809) Private in Sgt. PRYOR'S squad who enlisted with Clark in 1803. An excellent hunter, he also was the backup fiddler after CRUZATTE, and one of the three that the enlisted men nominated to replace Charles FLOYD as sergeant. He suffered one of the worst wounds on July 18, 1806, on the YELLOWSTONE RIVER. He fell from his horse onto a burned snag that pierced two inches into his thigh. His pain made riding impossible despite the men's making a bolster of clothing and hides he could lean back on while riding the gentlest horse. But, on July 30, Clark casually mentioned that Gibson could walk again and had just killed a BISON.

gill (*pronounced jill*) Liquid measure equal to ½ cup.

goat What the captains mistakenly called the PRONGHORN.

goat, mountain (*Oreamnos americanus*) White, shaggy-haired goats with short black horns, they live on steep mountain slopes, above timberline in summer but moving to lower sites in winter. Standing 3' to 3.5', they weigh from 100 to 300 pounds. The captains learned of them on August 24, 1805, when they asked the SHOSHONE INDIANS where they got the hides that looked like domestic sheep skins. The creatures then lived in the BITTERROOT MOUNTAINS in Shoshone home country. Neither Lewis nor Clark saw the animal on the hoof, and finally on April 10, 1806, they purchased a cap made from the hide of a mountain goat's head, horns remaining, and also bought the rest of the hide. It was expensive: the WISHRAM-WASCO INDIANS charged a knife for the cap and two ELK skins for the hide. Even as Lewis wrote the first scientific description of the animal, he continued to call it a sheep.

Goodrich, Silas (dates unknown) Private in Sgt. ORDWAY'S squad. Possibly transferred to the expedition from the regular army. He was the Corps' best fisherman.

goose, greater white-fronted (*Anser albifrons*) Lewis, misnaming it a BRANT, wrote the first scientific description and drew the bird's head on March 15, 1806, at FORT CLATSOP. It has yellow or orange feet and bill, is about 30" long, and winters in Mexico or the Gulf States, moving to Canadian tundra in summer.

Grand Detour *See* BIG BEND OF THE MISSOURI.

Gray, Robert Located the MOUTH of the COLUMBIA RIVER on the Pacific Ocean in May 1792. He named the river for his ship, the *Columbia Rediviva*.

greasewood (*Sarcobatus vermiculatus*) On May 11, 1805, Lewis first scientifically described a plant that was becoming a nuisance, which he called the "fleshey leafed thorn." The shrub tolerated alkaline soil and grew along the MISSOURI RIVER in today's eastern Montana. The wood was stiff, but held many "long, sha[r]p, strong" thorns. No animal seemed to eat it. It was a nuisance that continued to the MISSOURI'S HEAD-WATERS and beyond.

Great Bend In present North Dakota, where the MISSOURI RIVER turns south, now below Garrison DAM at the eastern end of Lake Sakakawea.

Great Chute Rapids about half a mile in extent, where the COLUMBIA RIVER was narrowed by rocks to a width of "150 paces." Today it is under the waters backed up by Bonneville DAM, upstream from Bridge of the Gods roughly between Stevenson, Washington, and Cascade Locks, Oregon.

The Corps reached the "Great Shute," as Clark wrote, on October 30, 1805. The next day, CRUZATTE and Joseph FIELD were put to work examining the rapids. The decision was to PORTAGE the baggage on land and haul the canoes through the water. On November 1, the men carried the baggage and the small CANOE over a rocky, slippery portage. They placed poles across the river rocks and let the four large canoes down. Even then, three boats were damaged. Immediately downstream was the CASCADES OF THE COLUMBIA.

Great Falls of the Columbia What the captains called CELILO FALLS.

Great Falls of the Missouri A series of five waterfalls, four of them now altered by DAMS and impounded water,

Great Falls of the Missouri in 1907
FROM ANACONDA COMPANY FILES, COURTESY OF MONTANA MAGAZINE

on the MISSOURI RIVER at today's city of Great Falls, Montana. Going upstream, as Lewis reached them, the names were the Great Falls (Ryan Dam, 1915), Crooked Falls, Colter Falls (submerged by water from Rainbow Dam), Handsome or Beautiful Falls (Rainbow Dam, 1910), and Upper Falls (Black Eagle Dam, 1891).

grog Originally made with rum on sailing ships, a mixture of half liquor and half water.

Gros Ventres of the Missouri What the captains sometimes called the HIDATSA Indians.

Gros Ventres of the Prairie What the captains sometimes called the Atsina Indians.

grouse The captains used this term generously for various species of birds. True grouse are chicken-like plump birds that nest on the ground. The following species were all new to science when the captains described them.
blue (Dendragapus obscurus) On July 21, 1805, near future Helena, Montana, Lewis recorded seeing two dark brown "pheasants" much larger than the ring-necked pheasant. He killed and studied one on August 1, near future Cardwell, Montana, and wrote his scientific description still calling it a pheasant. Blue grouse in the Rockies are dark, grayish brown blending into sooty black, 15½" to 21" long. They live in forests, moving to higher-elevation forests in winter.
Oregon ruffed (Bonasa umbellus togata) On September 20, 1805, the same day that a horse ran away permanently with Lewis's winter clothing, deep in the BITTERROOT MOUNTAINS, the captain

wrote science's first description of this grouse, calling it a pheasant. It lives in brushy woods, has a fan-shaped tail, and is 16"-19" long.
sage· (Centrocercus urophasianus) Lewis called it a "mountain cock," when he saw the first one on June 5, 1805, near today's Sweetgrass Hills in Montana. He

sage grouse
DONALD M. JONES

killed his first specimen on October 17, 1805, near the MOUTH of the SNAKE RIVER at today's Pasco, Washington, saying it was as large as a small turkey. Sage grouse live in open sagebrush country. The male has a spiked tail that he fans like a turkey's during courtship display. Males are much larger than females, 26"-30" long compared to 22"-23".
sharp-tailed (Tympanuchus phasianellus) Clark recorded the first sightings on September 5 and 12, 1804, correctly calling the birds grouse. They are light brown and white speckled, with pointed tails, and are 15"-20" long. They live at the forested edges of open PRAIRIE. Lewis never wrote a detailed scientific description, but sent JEFFERSON a live specimen via the RETURN PARTY. It didn't survive the trip.

Oregon ruffed grouse
BOB EVERTON

spruce (Falcipennis canadensis) Clark first noted this "pheasant" with a black tail when he killed four on September 13, 1805, as the Corps climbed upward from Lolo Hot Springs west of current Lolo, Montana. The males are black with some white speckling on the breast, and have a red comb above the eyes. Small, 15"-17", easily-approached spruce grouse live in wet conifer forests.

guns Men who transferred to the Corps of Discovery from other parts of the U.S. Army carried the government-issued muskets they already had. Fifteen rifles and sets of accessories came from the U.S. arsenal at HARPERS FERRY, then in Virginia. Some men carried personal weapons.

air rifle Lewis bought this from its inventor, Isaiah Lukens, in Philadelphia. It used compressed air rather than explosives to fire pellets; BB guns are a type of air gun. It seems to have been used only to amaze or entertain Indians, whose guns were muzzle-loaders like the Corps'.

blunderbuss Large shotgun with bell-shaped muzzle that fired buckshot. The Corps had two, on swivels, which they CACHED at the GREAT FALLS OF THE MISSOURI on the way west, and took back to St. Louis in 1806.

flintlock rifle
BOB EVERTON

flintlock See *rifle* in this section.

fusil Usually written *fusee* in the journals, after the French pronunciation. A shorter, lightweight long-barreled gun that could be rifled or smoothbore, and might have elaborate brass decoration on the stock. Clark wrote that on June 29, 1805, at the GREAT FALLS OF THE MISSOURI, he lost his "eligant fusee" in a flash flood.

muskets Most soldiers at the time were issued Model 1795 smoothbore (not *rifled*—see below) flintlock muskets, which could fire either .69-caliber bullets or buckshot. Muskets could be faster and easier to load than rifles.

muzzleloader A gun that is loaded from the barrel's opening (muzzle). All the Corps' guns were of this type.

pistols Lewis purchased a pair of small "pocket" pistols with "secret trigger" for ten dollars from gunsmith Robert Barnhill in PHILADELPHIA. He also obtained a pair of large flintlock handguns from the Harpers Ferry arsenal, "horseman's pistols" designed to fit a saddle holster.

rifle The Corps' guns were all flintlocks: pulling the trigger caused a flint to strike a spark that exploded gunpowder in the "priming pan" on the side, which in turn fired the charge that had been rammed down the barrel before the bullet was. Rifles, new technology at the time, had spiral grooves inside the gun barrel that gave the bullet greater range and more accuracy. Because they were slower and more difficult to load, rifles at the time were not yet in general use in the military.

In 1803, Lewis obtained 15 rifles at Harpers Ferry, and lack of detailed records (plus the captains' auctioning off their gear in St. Louis after the trek) leaves the exact model uncertain. Although a new Springfield rifle made just for the U.S. Army had been authorized, no records show that this .54-caliber Model 1803 was manufactured before 1804. Historians Gary E. MOULTON and Stephen Witte are among those who believe that the Corps carried prototypes of the Model 1803 "short rifle." Another prominent theory is that Lewis's 15 rifles were Model 1792s, in storage since General Anthony Wayne's 1792-1794 campaign against Indians of the Northwest Territory.

From Harpers Ferry, Lewis also stocked 15 each of powder horns, bullet molds, gun wipes, ball screws, and gun slings, plus 500 flints, along with replacement parts and repair tools that John SHIELDS put to good use.

Lewis, Clark, YORK, and some others supplied their own rifles, the long-barreled style called "Pennsylvania" or "Kentucky."

short rifle See *fusil* and *rifle* above.

swivel gun Mounted on the KEELBOAT, this was a small cannon that could be loaded with a one-pound ball or with multiple musket balls. The captains removed it from the keelboat and carried it from FORT MANDAN to the GREAT FALLS OF THE MISSOURI. They CACHED it there in 1805, then retrieved it and gave it to one of the Hidatsa chiefs on the way home the following year.

keelboat with swivel gun
ROBERT F. MORGAN

Guteridge, Guterage The captains' usual misspellings of GOODRICH.

Hadley's quadrant See OCTANT.

Hall, Hugh (ca. 1772-?) Private in Sgt. PRYOR'S squad. Transferred to the expedition from the army infantry. He and William WERNER were COURT MARTIALLED on May 17, 1805, for being AWOL at St. Charles, Missouri, and were sentenced to twenty-five lashes of the whip. The court recommended leniency and Clark did not carry out the punishment. Six weeks later, on the night of June 28-29, Hall broke into the whiskey supply and got drunk. The next day, both he and John COLLINS were court martialled in camp at future Kansas City, Kansas. Hall was sentenced to—and received—fifty lashes of the whip. Collins, because he was the sentinel on duty, received harsher punishment for failing at guarding.

Harpers Ferry Today in West Virginia, which broke off from Virginia in 1863. Lewis obtained supplies from the army arsenal here, and also shipped in goods purchased in PHILADELPHIA.

He first was here from mid-March to mid-April 1803, selecting rifles (*see* GUNS) and knives, and ordering other metal items (including the IRON BOAT frame and waterproof gunpowder canisters made of lead that would be molded into bullets when emptied) to be manufactured.

Lewis returned to Harpers Ferry early in July, where he tested the guns, inspected the iron boat with pleasure, and arranged to ship the supplies on to Pittsburgh.

The arsenal is best known for the failed 1859 raid by abolitionist John Brown and his followers, who believed they would incite a slave rebellion with stolen armaments. Although the building Lewis visited was destroyed in 1861 by Confederate troops, the story of his visits is told at Harpers Ferry National Historical Park today.

Hat Rock Rises above today's Lake Wallula on the Columbia east of Umatilla, Oregon. The Corps passed and named it for its shape on October 18, 1805. The following spring, on April 27, the captains did not mention Hat Rock in the journals as they passed it again. Today Hat Rock State Park surrounds the rock.

headwaters Where a creek or river begins. *See also* THREE FORKS OF THE MISSOURI RIVER.

Hidatsa Indians *See* MANDAN AND HIDATSA INDIANS.

hominy *See* CORN.

horses *See* BITTERROOT MOUNTAINS, CELILO FALLS, MOCCASINS, NEZ PERCE INDIANS, Nathaniel PRYOR, SALMON RIVER, SHOSHONE INDIANS.

Howard, Thomas (1779-?) Private in Sgt. PRYOR'S squad. Transferred to the expedition from the army infantry. He was COURT MARTIALLED at FORT MANDAN on February 10, 1805, for climbing over the 18' stockade wall, thus showing the neighbors how easy it was to do. His sentence was fifty lashes of the whip, but mercy was recommended and so Lewis cancelled it. This was the last court martial the Corps saw.

huckleberry *See* BERRIES.

Illinois Phrased as "the Illinois" in the journals, this meant the general area of today's state of Illinois, north of the Ohio River, west of Indiana Territory. It was unorganized frontier until Illinois Territory was created in 1809.

imposthume The captains' term for an abscess.

iron boat An invention by Lewis that he called his "experiment." At HARPERS FERRY arsenal, he experimented with two designs before choosing the one to be built. The 36'-long iron frame then was constructed to his specifications. It weighed 99 pounds and was taken all the way to the GREAT FALLS OF THE MISSOURI before he had it put together, fitted with wooden seats, and covered with twenty-eight ELK and four BISON hides. It was to carry four tons of men and cargo. Unfortunately, back in Virginia, Lewis had wrongly assumed that pine pitch for caulking the stitched seams would be available everywhere on the continent. With none available around the falls, he concocted a substitute mixture that peeled off the seams as soon as it dried. When he launched the boat on July 9, 1805, it sank—leaving him "mortifyed not a little." The frame was CACHED, but the journals do not mention the expedition's digging it up on the return trip.

jay Raucous, omnivorous relative of crows and MAGPIES. Species new to science at the time of the Lewis and Clark Expedition include:
Clark's nutcracker (Nucifraga columbiana) Lives in the higher parts of the ROCKY MOUNTAINS. First record-

Clark's nutcracker
BOB EVERTON

ed for science by Clark at the SALMON RIVER'S HEADWATERS on August 22, 1805, as a type of "woodpecker" the size of a robin, which ate seeds. It is 11"-12" long. A later ornithologist named it for the captain.

pinyon (Gymnorhinus cyanocephalus) Lewis first shot at and missed this bird, but wrote about it in some detail, on August 1, 1805, near today's Cardwell, Montana. It has no crest and is robin-sized at 9"-11¾", colored dull blue all over. Pinyon jays range from pine and juniper forests into sagebrush.

Steller's (Cyanocitta stelleri) Lewis first wrote of it during the perilous BITTERROOT MOUNTAINS crossing on September 20, 1805, as pigeon-sized but acting like a jay. At FORT CLATSOP in December, he wrote the detailed scientific description. Slightly larger than the blue jay at 12"-13½", it has a black head and crest, dull blue body, and deeper blue wings. Lives in conifer forests.

Jefferson, Thomas (1743-1826) Third president of the United States (1801-1808), he was as much a scientist as he was an American patriot and a politician. In the 1790s, Jefferson was twice involved in efforts to organize a MISSOURI RIVER exploring expedition. (Lewis, in fact, had volunteered to lead one of these.) As president, Jefferson was able to make the LOUISIANA PURCHASE—largely to prevent the land's being taken by a European nation. He saw the Lewis and Clark Expedition also as a chance to gather much information for world scientists about the center of North America. Besides requiring them to map the rivers, he assigned the captains to note the land's agricultural potential, obtain Indian vocabularies and information on religion and customs, and bring back specimens and scientific written descriptions of animals and plants unknown in Europe and the eastern United States.

Jefferson River One of the three streams that form the MISSOURI RIVER at Three Forks, Montana. Correctly believing it to be the tributary beginning highest in the mountains, they named it for Thomas JEFFERSON. The Corps traveled upstream on it from July 30, 1805, to August 4, when Lewis's advance party reached its HEADWATERS and moved onto its tributary the BEAVERHEAD RIVER. *See also* PHILANTHROPY RIVER, PHILOSOPHY RIVER, WISDOM RIVER.

Thomas Jefferson, from a U.S. Capitol mural
REPRODUCED FROM THE COLLECTIONS OF THE LIBRARY OF CONGRESS

jerked meat Freshly butchered meat cut into strips and hung on a wooden framework to dry in the air or above a fire. This preserved it. The Corps of Discovery probably salted the meat, but Indians did not.

journals The captains used bound books and other notebooks to make their field notes—in duplicate. These were carried in tin boxes to protect the ink from water splashes. In spring 1805, they sent the first batch back to Thomas JEFFERSON via the RETURN PARTY. In 1817-1818, most of the handwritten journals were given to the American Philosophical Society, PHILADELPHIA, where they remain.

Reproduction of one of Clark's journals, which has an elkskin cover J. AGEE

Each sergeant was required to keep a journal from the day the trip began, and all but one of these were eventually published, including FLOYD'S very short one. The fate of Sgt. PRYOR'S journal is unknown. Privates WHITE-HOUSE and FRAZER voluntarily kept journals; the former has been published and the latter lost. *See also:* Nicholas BIDDLE, Elliot COUES, Gary E. MOULTON, Reuben Gold THWAITES.

Jusseaume, René Having worked as a scout for George Rogers CLARK on the Northwest frontier, he was an independent trader living with his MANDAN wife and their children in MITUTANKA when Clark met him on October 27, 1804. He had been accepted among the Mandans for fifteen years and at once offered his services as an Mandan interpreter. He was not very good at the job, though, and the captains also were not fond of his personality. In 1806, when Chief SHEHEKE agreed to go to Washington, D.C., he insisted that the JUSSEAUME family also go, which they did.

Kaw Indians The captains' term for the Kansas Indians.

keelboat This was a common form of river transportation at the time, and Pittsburgh, Pennsylvania, where Lewis had his built, was the nation's keelboat-building center. Keelboats can travel in relatively shallow water, an important feature in those days before DAMS and locks controlled river depths. Usually, they were about 70' long. The Corps' keelboat was only 55' long and 8' wide, and had 22 oars and a mast for raising a sail. It had a cabin at the stern (back) with a small deck atop it. The hold was 31' long. Storage compartments around the deck had lids that could be raised as protection against attack.

Clark sketched the keelboat in his journal, and a replica based on his drawings is exhibited at Lewis and Clark State Park near Onawa, Iowa.

Kentucky, Nine Young Men from Clark recruited at least seven men from around Louisville, Kentucky, and Clarksville, Indiana Territory, where he lived. They were all frontiersmen, which followed Thomas JEFFERSON'S advice that the captains not take "young gentlemen" who weren't familiar with living in the woods. When Lewis arrived on the KEELBOAT, he seems to have had two men on board for a try-out.

The men called the "Nine Young Men" are: William BRATTON, John COLTER (probably arrived with Lewis), Joseph and Reubin FIELD, Charles FLOYD, George GIBSON, Nathaniel PRYOR, George SHANNON (probably arrived with Lewis), and John SHIELDS.

Killamucks The captains' name for Tillamook Indians.

kinnikinnick See BERRIES: *bearberry.*

What the keelboat probably looked like
BOB EVERTON

knives At the U.S. arsenal at HARPERS FERRY, Lewis obtained fifteen "scalping" knives for members of the expedition. (Men transferring to the Corps from other army units would bring the gear they already had.) These had wooden handles and curved, pointed blades made of carbon steel, a soft steel that is easily resharpened. Because these could not be replaced, if a man left his behind, he had to return to last night's camp, retrieve it, and catch up with the advancing Corps.

Lewis purchased four drawing knives, which had a slightly curved blade with a handle at each end. The user drew, or pulled, it toward himself to peel bark from logs or further smooth and shape them.

Among the "Indian presents" were four dozen butcher knives, which had a wide blade with a rounded point.

drawing knife
BOB EVERTON

Kooskee or **Kooskooskee River**
See CLEARWATER RIVER.

Labiche, Francois

Labiche, Francois (dates unknown) Private in Sgt. PRYOR'S squad, an experienced Indian trader, good boatman, and translator thought to be of French and Omaha heritage. He enlisted in the army in order to join the expedition.

larboard The left side of a boat as one faces forward in it. In standard usage at the time, also the left side of a river as one faces downstream, but Clark often wrote "larboard" when he simply meant the left bank compared to his position.

latitude In the Corps' case, how far north of the equator they were. "North latitude" is given in degrees, based on 90° in the quarter circle from Earth's equator (0°) to 90° at the North Pole, plus minutes and seconds. A "minute" is one sixtieth of a degree, and a second is one sixtieth of a minute, not referring to time in this case. The latitude of today's Stanton, North Dakota, site of MAHAWHA, is written 35°50'12"N, meaning 35 degrees, 50 minutes, and 12 seconds north of the equator.

laudanum A tincture (solution) of 10% opium and 90% alcohol, given in small doses for pain relief.

Lepage, Jean Baptiste (dates unknown) The captains enlisted this former member of the platoon of hired French boatmen on November 3, 1804, at Fort Mandan. He replaced John NEWMAN. Lepage was French Canadian and had spent time with the Cheyenne Indians.

Lemhi Pass In the BEAVERHEAD MOUNTAINS at 7,339' elevation, east of today's Tendoy, Idaho. On the westward trip, members of the Corps crossed it five times going between TRAVELERS' REST and SHOSHONE INDIAN villages as they prepared for and crossed the Rockies.

Lemhi Shoshone Indians *See* SHOSHONE INDIANS.

Lewis, Meriwether (1774-1809) Raised near Charlottesville, Virginia, in a family known to— but not in the same social circles as—Thomas JEFFERSON. He became a captain while serving in the army in the Ohio Valley and Northwest Territory in the 1790s, and kept that rank when he became President Jefferson's private secretary in 1801.

Named governor of Louisiana Territory following the expedition, Lewis did not handle political situations well. Further, the U.S. Congress also was looking into why the expedition cost more than planned. Lewis, a lifelong sufferer of depres-

Meriwether Lewis, by Charles Willson Peale
COURTESY INDEPENDENCE NATIONAL PARK, PHILADELPHIA

sion, was on the Natchez Trace heading to Washington, D.C., in 1809 to answer Congress when he took his own life.

Lewis and Clark Pass Lewis and his MARIAS RIVER exploration party crossed this 7,452' pass northeast of present Lincoln, Montana, on the CONTINENTAL DIVIDE on July 7, 1806. Clark never saw the pass later named to honor both captains.

Lewis's woodpecker
BOB EVERTON

Lewis's woodpecker (*Melanerpes lewis*) A large woodpecker of the western U.S. mountains and Canada, first described scientifically by Lewis on July 20, 1805, and May 27, 1806, but named for him by a later ornithologist. It has a black back and head, gray collar and red face, and is the only North American woodpecker to have a pinkish-red belly. It is 10½" to 11" long.

licorice, wild (*Glycyrrhiza lepidota*) SACAGAWEA gathered this plant on May 8, 1805, when the Corps encountered hillsides covered with it west of the Milk River in future Montana. Lewis did not write a scientific description, but he collected specimens that botanist Frederick Pursh later recognized as wild licorice. The plant was cultivated in Europe, but did not grow in the eastern U.S. at the time. Native people chewed the roots to ease toothache and sooth the stomach and intestines, and chewed the leaves to make a paste to put on horses' sore backs.

liniment An ointment or liquid rubbed on the skin to ease muscle tightness or ache.

Lolo Trail North of and roughly parallel to present U.S. Highway 12 from Lolo, Montana, to Kooskia, Idaho. The trail the NEZ PERCE INDIANS used to cross the BITTERROOT MOUNTAINS via Lolo Pass to hunt for BISON east of the ROCKY MOUNTAINS. TOBY guided the Corps westward over this trail, September 11-21, 1805, and five unnamed young Nez Perce men guided them back, June 26-29, 1806. In 1877, Chief Joseph led his band of Nez Perce east over the same trail trying to escape being forced from their Idaho homeland to a Washington reservation.

Long Camp Some modern historians' name for CAMP CHOPUNNISH.

longitude Measurement, in degrees, of how far east or west around Earth a location is from the prime meridian, an imaginary north-south line through the site of the Royal Observatory Greenwich in England. For the captains, longitude was in degrees west (written "W") of the imaginary 0° line. To figure longitude with the equipment they had, a captain had to take multiple celestial observations over several hours of clear sky, with the help of three assistants. He had to adjust the figures for refraction, or the bending of light by Earth's atmosphere, and other factors. Just as important as these observations was knowing the exact time of each one. (Their CHRONOMETER stopped more than once, and the captains could reset it only by deciding when the sun was "exactly" overhead, marking noon.) Charts had to be referred to, and mathematical formulas figured. On January 14, 1805, at FORT MANDAN, the captains calculated their longitude based on observations made at the beginning and the end of a lunar eclipse. Their results were both 99°22'45.3"W and 99°26'45"W. The actual position, according to historian Gary E. MOULTON, is 101°27'W.

Long Narrows *See* THE DALLES.

Lookout, Clark's, and **Lewis's Lookout** Two sites near—and often confused with—each other north of present Dillon, Montana. Lewis, traveling ahead in search of the SHOSHONE INDIANS, climbed a cliff about 24 miles north of Dillon on August 10, 1805, to see what lay in his path. Lewis's Lookout today is on private land but can be viewed from public roadway. Behind with the main party, Clark climbed a rocky hill 1 mile from Dillon on August 13, 1805. Today interpretive signs mark Clark's Lookout State Park at the site.

Louisiana Purchase To the French, "Upper Louisiana" was the land west of the Mississippi that was drained by the Missouri, Red, and Arkansas river systems—and "Lower Louisiana" was approximately today's state of Louisiana. France had claimed the land, named it for King Louis XIV, sent voyageurs to trap and trade with Indians for rich furs, but settlement was nearly nonexistent. Through war, France lost control to Spain, and then obtained Louisiana once again by treaties in 1800 and 1801. Meanwhile, more and more U.S. citizens were moving onto the frontier west of the Appalachian Mountains, toward the Mississippi River that was their nation's western edge. President JEFFERSON entered his first term know-

ing that whatever nation controlled the Mississippi at New Orleans could cut off American river trade.

In 1803, Napoleon, governing France, was moving toward war against Britain, and being urged by his own ministers to sell Louisiana to fund the effort. American ambassador Robert Livingston was joined in Paris by Jefferson's emissary James Madison, to try to buy New Orleans, Florida, and the southern parts of future Alabama and Mississippi. Instead they were offered the entire Louisiana, and negotiated a total price of $15 million, signing the treaty on April 30. And so 828,000 square miles were added to the United States, as the public learned when the news was published on July 4, 1803.

Remote from France and Spain, Louisiana had not formally been moved from Spain's control. On March 9, 1804, representing the United States, Capt. Amos Stoddard officially transferred Upper Louisiana from Spain to France. After allowing the French flag to wave over ST. LOUIS for a day, he completed the transfer from France to the United States. Neither Lewis nor Clark mentioned the ceremonies in his journal.

Louisiana Purchase

BOB EVERTON

Loup Indians The French word for "wolf" was what the captains called the Pawnee Indians, who lived in northeastern Nebraska where the Loup River flowed into the PLATTE RIVER.

Lower Portage Camp Downstream from the GREAT FALLS OF THE MISSOURI, at the MOUTH of today's Belt Creek in Montana.

McNeal, Hugh (dates unknown) Private in Sgt. FLOYD'S squad. Possibly transferred to the expedition from the regular army.

black-billed magpie
DONALD M. JONES

Madison River *See* THREE FORKS OF THE MISSOURI RIVER.

magpie, black-billed (*Pica pica*) Known in Europe, magpies had not been recorded in North America until Lewis wrote about one on September 16, 1804. It is 17½" to 22" long, with a long tail (9½"-12") that is diamond-shaped in flight. Its deep black feathers have a green iridescence on the back and bluish iridescence on the wings. It lives on rangeland, forest edges, waterways, farms, and in towns.

Mahahas The captains' name for HIDATSA INDIANS.

Mahars The captains' name for Omaha Indians.

Mahawha Southernmost of the three HIDATSA villages near FORT MANDAN, it stood where the Mercer County Courthouse, in Stanton, North Dakota, does today. *See also* MANDAN AND HIDATSA INDIANS.

malaria Now the most widespread illness in the world, it is caused by the tiny parasite *Plasmodium,* which is carried by MOSQUITOES. In the expedition's era, no one knew what caused it, but people suspected it had something to do with the air around swamps, and still waters along rivers that included the Ohio, Mississippi, and Missouri—which are great mosquito-breeding places. Malarial attacks of recurrent chills and fever can have fatal complications affecting the kidneys, lungs, spinal cord, and brain. Quinine is the effective treatment; natural quinine occurs in PERUVIAN BARK.

Mandan and Hidatsa Indians Near today's Stanton, North Dakota, where the Knife River flows into the MISSOURI RIVER, were two Mandan and three Hidatsa villages that were a well known trading center visited by Indians and whites. Pierre CRUZATTE had visited them before the expedition. The captains planned to spend winter 1804-1805 in the area, and did build

Mandan earth lodge
BOB EVERTON

45

FORT MANDAN there. The agricultural Mandans had moved near the more warlike Hidatsas after losing many members to a smallpox epidemic two decades before the Corps visited. They built large earth lodges that housed several families each, and raised squash, beans, and CORN. Today the Hidatsa and Mandan—with former enemy the ARIKARA—form the Three Affiliated Tribes of Fort Berthold Indian Reservation, North Dakota. *See also* MAHAWHA, METAHARTA, MENETARRA, MITUTANKA, RUPTÁRE.

Marias River Tributary of the MISSOURI RIVER in north-central Montana. As the Corps came up the Missouri to it on June 2, 1805, the Marias was equal in size to the Missouri. No informant had mentioned such a "fork" in the Missouri. All the men, including riverman CRUZATTE, thought it was the Missouri because it was muddy like the river they had been traveling. Because the other "fork" was clearer, the captains correctly thought it the main Missouri, which should be clear because it came out of the Rockies not many miles away. Rather than force the men to follow them, the captains had the main party encamp; Clark led a small group up the Missouri, and Lewis another up the Marias. They returned with the same opinion, and still the men did not agree. Lewis then took his turn going up the *Missouri* to travel until he could find proof. About ten miles beyond where Clark had had to turn back, Lewis found the GREAT FALLS OF THE MISSOURI, the expected landmark.

On the return trip, Lewis led a small group from the Great Falls to the higher reaches and tributaries of the Marias in July 1806 to see how far north the stream began, because this would extend the LOUISIANA PURCHASE northward. Bad weather made observations to figure LATITUDE impossible, leading Lewis to name his farthest point CAMP DISAPPOINTMENT. As the men turned toward the Missouri River, they met a small group of BLACKFEET INDIAN warriors, with bloody results.

marten (*Martes americana*) Nocturnal, tree-climbing mammal, trapped for its yellowish-brown fur. About 15" long with about 8" long, thickly furred, dark-brown tail. They live in fir, spruce, and hemlock forests.

marten
DONALD M. JONES

Ma-too-ton ka *See* MITUTANKA.

meadowlark, western *(Sternella neglecta)* New to science when Clark first mentioned it on September 25, 1804, near present Vermillion, South Dakota. It is a plumpish brown bird with bright yellow vest and flute-like, multi-note song, 9" long. It lives in western grasslands from Mexico to Canada.

medicine chest A fitted wooden box that held glass bottles of medicines, a mortar and pestle, and surgical and dental instruments. Lewis purchased two, one of walnut and the other of pine, from Gillaspy and Smith, pharmacists, in PHILADELPHIA on May 26, 1803. He stocked them with $46.52 ($516.89 today) worth of medications and instruments.

Menetarra Third HIDATSA village up the Knife River from FORT MANDAN. *See also* MANDAN AND HIDATSA INDIANS.

mess Group of soldiers assigned to cook and eat together; they were given one kettle to cook in. The assigned cook had to prepare or preserve fresh meat promptly, and clean the utensils. In return, he was excused from guard duty.

Metaharta Second Hidatsa village up the Knife River from FORT MANDAN. SACAGAWEA lived here after being captured by the Hidatsas in future Montana. The captains believed that BLACK MOCCASIN was its chief. *See also* MANDAN AND HIDATSA INDIANS.

Minitarees The captains' name for Hidatsa Indians.

Minetares of Fort de Prairies The captains' name for Atsina Indians.

Missouri Breaks Land in central Montana upstream from today's Fort Peck DAM to Virgelle, east of Fort Benton. Rough, eroded, largely sandstone bluffs rise from 100' to 300' above the MISSOURI RIVER, which flows deep, narrow, and swift. On May 8, 1805, the Corps passed and named (for its color) the Milk River in future Montana. They had entered the Missouri Breaks, a land of "visionary inchantment" but very rough slogging. The narrow river banks were covered with clay-filled gumbo mud so sticky it pulled off the men's MOCCASINS when they had to CORDELLE the boats. Mixed into the mud were many sharp stones. Lewis later wrote that the men's "labor is incredibly painful and great, yet

western meadowlark
DONALD M. JONES

47

those faithful fellows bear it without a murmur." It took until June 2 to travel the 523 river miles through the area.

In 2000, 149 river miles surrounded by 377,346 acres was named as the Upper Missouri River Breaks National Monument. This area extends upstream from U.S. Highway 191 to U.S. Highway 87. The Missouri in this area had been named a National Wild and Scenic River in 1976. *See also* WHITE CLIFFS.

Missouri River The Corps of Discovery traveled the Missouri from May 14 to October 26, 1804, to the MANDAN AND HIDATSA villages, and April 7 to July 25, 1805, when they reached its HEADWATERS at the THREE FORKS OF THE MISSOURI. By Clark's reckoning, the Missouri's length was 2,848 river miles. The expedition's main assignment was to map the Missouri and streams that flowed into it. The farther away were the headwaters of its tributaries, the bigger the LOUISIANA PURCHASE was. Therefore, on the return trip in 1806, the captains split up and Lewis went north to see how far north the tributary MARIAS RIVER and its tributaries began. Clark explored the tributary YELLOWSTONE RIVER to see whether it was navigable for commercial purposes.

Today's Missouri River is very different from the river the captains traveled. DAMS for hydropower and flood control have created lakes that cover their riverbank campsites.

The Yellowstone River (left) flows into the Missouri River in North Dakota
LARRY MAYER

Mitutanka Closer Mandan Indian village to FORT MANDAN, about half a mile upstream on the southern side of the MISSOURI RIVER. SHEHEKE and Little Crow were its chiefs. *See also* MANDAN AND HIDATSA INDIANS.

moccasins For most of the trip, the men made their own or bought moccasins from Indians. Because these wore out quickly, they made extras during their longer stops; at FORT CLATSOP they stitched up about ten pairs

moccasins
J. AGEE

apiece to start the return trip. In 1806, on the YELLOWSTONE RIVER, the horses' feet were very sore from the rocky soil, so Clark had the men make BISON-skin moccasins for the animals.

mosquito (*Aedes vexans*) The torturer of people and beasts during warm months was more dangerous than they knew, being a potential source of MALARIA. Clouds of mosquitoes were so thick that at times Clark waved branches before him as he walked along. The men smeared BEAR grease on their bodies to try to stop the biting, and at night set smoky fires to keep mosquitoes off themselves, SEAMAN—and horses, when they had them.

Moulton, Gary E. Editor of the definitive edition of *The Journals of the Lewis & Clark Expedition*, which presents, collates, annotates, and indexes all available expedition maps and journals. Publication extended from the 1980s into the 21st century.

mouth Where a creek or river ends by flowing into another or into an ocean.

muskrat (*Ondatra zibethica*) Water mammal trapped then and now for its dense fur. The body is 10"-14" long, with a hairless, scaly tail of 8"-10". They build houses in shallow water, or dig dens in river banks.

muzzleloader *See* GUNS.

naming of sites The captains recorded Indian names for their "milestones," the geographical features around them, if they learned them. On October 22, 1805, Clark wrote "haveing no Indian name that we could find out…we think it best to leave the name-ing of [islands in the Columbia River] untill our return." In the process of assigning names, the captains labeled at least one feature for each man, woman, baby, and dog of the Corps. Some received more than one such honor.

mosquito
ROBERT F. MORGAN

49

naming of sites

River names given by the captains that honor members of the Corps *and* are still in use today are: CLARK FORK RIVER (Montana); CLARKS FORK YELLOWSTONE RIVER (Montana); Floyd River (Iowa), Pryor's Creek (Montana), Shannon's River (South Dakota), Shields River (Montana).

Names honoring members that are no longer used, with modern name and location, are:

Bratton's Creek—Bridger Creek (Montana); Bratton's River—Timber Creek (Montana)

[Charbonneau, Jean Baptiste "Pompy"] Pompy's Tower—POMPEYS PILLAR (Montana); Baptiste's Creek—Pillar Creek (Montana)

[T.] Charbonneau's Creek—Bear Den Creek (North Dakota); Charbonneau's River—Cherry Creek (Montana)

Clark's River—Bitterroot River (Montana); Point William—Tongue Point (Oregon)

Collins Creek—Lolo Creek (Idaho; separate from the Lolo Creek in Montana)

Colter Creek—Potlatch River (Idaho)

Cruzatte's River—Wind River (Washington)

Drouillard's River—Palouse River (Washington)

Joseph Field River—Charbonneau Creek (North Dakota)

R. Field Valley—Boulder River Valley (Montana)

Frazer's Creek—South Boulder River (Montana)

Gass's Creek—Crow Creek (Montana)

Gibson's Creek—Sutherland Creek (Montana); Gibson's River—Cabin Creek (Montana)

Goodrich's Island—Dry Island (Montana)

Hall's Strand Creek—Tobacco Creek (North Dakota); Hall's River—Cow Gulch (Montana)

Howard's Creek—Sixteenmile Creek (Montana)

Labiche's River—Sarpy Creek (Montana); River Labiche—Hood River (Oregon)

Lepage's River—John Day River (Oregon)

Lewis's River—Lemhi and Salmon rivers (when temporarily thought to be the upper reaches of the Snake); SNAKE RIVER (Idaho/Washington); Tucannon River (Washington); Meriwether Point (site of Astoria, Oregon)

McNeal's Creek—Blacktail Deer Creek (Montana)

Ordway's Creek—Little Prickly Pear Creek (Montana)

Potts Creek—Spring Creek (Montana)

Pryor's Creek—Spokane Creek (Montana); Pryor's River—Dry Creek (Montana)

Sacagawea River—Crooked Creek (Montana)

Shannon's River—Fly Creek (Montana)

Seaman's Creek—Monture Creek (Montana)

Shields River—Highwood Creek (Montana)

Thompson's Creek—Birch Creek (Montana)

Weiser's Creek—Fourchette Creek (Montana)

Werner's Creek—Clearwater River (Montana; separate from the Clearwater River of Idaho); Werner's Run—Duck Creek (Valley County, Montana)

Whitehouse Creek—Duck Creek (Broadwater County, Montana)

Willard's Creek—Grasshopper Creek (Montana)

Windsor's Creek—Muggins Creek (Montana); Windsor's River—Cow Creek (Montana)

York's Dry River—Custer Creek (Montana)

navigation *See* SEXTANT, COURSES.

Netul River The Indian name, which the Corps used, for today's Lewis and Clark River in Oregon, where they built FORT CLATSOP.

Newman, John (ca. 1785-1838) Private originally in Sgt. FLOYD'S squad. Transferred to the expedition from the army infantry. After being convicted on October 13, 1804, of seriously mutinous talk, he was given seventy-five lashes of the whip, banished from the Corps and assigned to hard labor over the winter of 1804-1805 then sent back with the RETURN PARTY. After good behavior during the winter, Newman asked to be reinstated. Lewis refused, but after the expedition included Newman in the list of men for whom he requested rewards from Congress.

Nez Perce Indians Living on the west side of the CONTINENTAL DIVIDE (in future Idaho, Oregon, and Washington) and allies of the SHOSHONE INDIANS, they welcomed and fed Clark's starving advance party when it came out of the BITTERROOT MOUNTAINS on September 20, 1805. Chiefs Twisted Hair and Tetoharsky went with the Corps down the COLUMBIA RIVER, introducing them as far as they could speak the local language (CELILO FALLS). The Nez Perce cared for the Corps' horse herd over the winter of 1805-1806 (great horsemen, the tribe developed the Appaloosa horse breed). Eager to leave the rainy Pacific coast climate, the Corps arrived back in Nez Perce country too early to cross the Rockies in spring 1806, and set up CAMP CHOPUNNISH. Five young Nez Perce men guided the Corps back over the tribe's LOLO TRAIL on June 26-29, 1806. The Nez Perce gradually ceded land to the United States until 1877,

when a forced move to their current reservation at Lapwai, Idaho, was resisted by Wallowa Valley (Oregon) Nez Perce under Chief Joseph. This band attempted to flee to Canada over several months but were defeated just miles from the border. *See also* THE DALLES.

Nez Perce Trail *See* LOLO TRAIL.

Nine Young Men *See* KENTUCKY, NINE YOUNG MEN FROM.

niter Potassium nitrate, or saltpeter, increases perspiration and urination. It was one of Benjamin RUSH'S many purgative medicines.

Northwest Today called the Old Northwest. At the time of the Revolutionary War, it was part of the frontier north of the OHIO RIVER and east of the Mississippi, the future states of Ohio (admitted 1803), Indiana (1816), Illinois (1818), Michigan (1837), Wisconsin (1848), and part of Minnesota (1858).

octant
J. AGEE

octant Instrument with a curved scale that is one eighth of a circle, or 45°, used to sight a celestial object and measure its ALTITUDE from the horizon to obtain the user's LATITUDE. *See also* SEXTANT.

Ohio River Lewis traveled its entire length in 1803, beginning on August 31 at the HEADWATERS in Pittsburgh, stopping at Clarksville, Indiana, to pick up Clark and the "Nine Young Men from KENTUCKY," and on to its MOUTH on the Mississippi River. The Ohio was exceptionally low that year, and the KEELBOAT often had to be CORDELLED over rocks. Today, twenty DAMS produce power and control water level for navigation.

Ordway, John (ca. 1775-ca. 1817) Sergeant. Transferred to the expedition from the army infantry, the only sergeant who was regular army. The captains put him in charge of CAMP DUBOIS when both were absent, and he remained one of the most dependable hands. On the return trip in 1806, he was in charge of the canoe party that split off at the THREE FORKS OF THE MISSOURI to return by river to the GREAT FALLS OF THE MISSOURI, dig up CACHES, and, meeting some of the men who had gone overland with Lewis, portage baggage around the falls.

otter, sea (*Enhydra lutris*) Lewis wrote on February 23, 1806, that the fur of this five-foot-long salt-water mammal was the "most delicious fur in the world." It is, in fact, the thickest of any animal.

They once lived from Mexico to Alaska, choosing shallow coastal kelp beds; when resting, they wrap themselves in kelp for anchorage. Males weigh up to ninety pounds. Some survive off California and Alaska, but the last Oregon sea otter was killed in 1906.

Pahkees What the captains called the BLACKFEET INDIANS. It was from the SHOSHONE word for "enemy."

Pania Indians Pawnee Indians.

Patterson, Robert (1743-1824) Mathematician who refined Lewis's skills after his training with ELLICOTT. Lewis studied with him, Benjamin RUSH, and two others from May 10 through June, 1803. On September 8, 1803, at Wheeling (then Virginia), Lewis met William Ewing Patterson, a physician who was Robert's son. Although the young doctor agreed to go along on the expedition, he failed to return to the KEELBOAT for departure.

sea otter
BOB EVERTON

peace medals The captains carried silver and copper medals in different sizes and two types of designs. These were given to chiefs according to their rank—as Lewis and Clark perceived it. One design, in three sizes, carried a profile of Thomas JEFFERSON, with a picture on the other side of two hands shaking, and the words "peace and friendship." A smaller medal that had been created before Jefferson was president, called the "seasons" medal, showed the occupations that Indians were supposed to take up: loom weaving, tending livestock, and planting wheat.

The United States had learned this custom from European nations. At FORT MANDAN, the captains spoke sharply to British fur traders who were passing out their medals while the captains wintered there.

peace pipe Smoking together was one of the formal ways that Indian nations greeted visitors and began meetings and ceremonies. Clark used it to indicate he came in peace on the COLUMBIA, when a fearful Umatilla Indian village hid from him on October 19, 1805. He sat out in the open in sight of their lodges and put down his GUN to prepare his pipe, showing his peaceful intentions.

peace pipe
BOB EVERTON

pelican, American white (*Pelecanus erythrorhynchos*) Pelicans lived east of the Appalachians, but Lewis was very surprised to see them on the MISSOURI RIVER on August 8, 1804, when a flock covered the whole river near present Onawa, Iowa, and Decatur, Nebraska.

pemmican Indians mixed dried meat with animal fat, dried roots, and/or BERRIES. Cakes of pemmican were the original "energy bar," a high protein food that could be stored all winter, eaten without heating, and easily carried for travel. The Corps first tasted this food when the Teton SIOUX on September 26, 1804, served pemmican as part of a meal.

permanent party Expedition members who went from FORT MANDAN to FORT CLATSOP and back to ST. LOUIS. The army party included, besides the co-captains, three sergeants and twenty-three privates. Traveling with them were the civilians YORK, interpreters SACAGAWEA and Toussaint CHARBONNEAU (with their baby), and George DROUILLARD. The original plan had been for some of the army men to go home by ship, because the captains knew that trading ships put in along the Pacific coast. By the time the Corps reached the Pacific, though, the captains had decided that they needed all hands to pass through certain Indian lands on the way home. Just as well, because they had missed the last of the season's trading ships.

Peruvian bark The dried bark of the cinchona tree, a native of Peru, was used to treat chills and fever. Its active ingredient, quinine, was not yet understood, but at the time Peruvian bark was known as a treatment for MALARIA.

Philadelphia

Philadelphia United States capital from the Revolution until 1800, and also the new nation's center of learning. The city counted about 81,000 residents when Lewis arrived in 1803 for specialized training from Robert PATTERSON, Benjamin RUSH, and Caspar WISTAR. Lewis also obtained 3,500 pounds of supplies—including finely crafted medical, navigational, and cartographic instruments—for the expedition, from private merchants and the SCHUYLKILL ARSENAL.

Philanthropy River Today's Ruby River in Montana, a tributary of the JEFFERSON RIVER. The captains named it for one of Thomas JEFFERSON'S virtues.

Philosophy River Today's Willow Creek in Montana, a tributary of the JEFFERSON RIVER. The captains named it for one of Thomas JEFFERSON'S virtues.

Phoca Rock On November 2, 1805, Clark described a rock in the middle of the COLUMBIA RIVER that rose about 100' above the river. The captains named it using the Greek word for seal, because they were seeing harbor seals in the area. Today, because of DAMS' having raised the Columbia, Phoca

Rock reaches only about 30' above the surface. See also SEAL, HARBOR.

Pillar Rock The Corps of Discovery camped on the Washington side of the COLUMBIA RIVER on November 7, 1805, opposite Pillar Rock, at the upper end of the Columbia ESTUARY. After reaching the Pacific on the Columbia's future Washington side, they went back upstream to Pillar Rock, camping near the same spot on November 25 and crossing to the Columbia's south side the following day. Today a navigational light tops Pillar Rock.

pilot One who could "read" a river and determine the best channel to follow, or who was familiar with a particular stretch of river that he guided boats through. Lewis hired pilots on the OHIO RIVER, CRUZATTE was the best pilot among the Corps, and sometimes local Indians were hired.

pirogue An open boat like an oversized dugout canoe, which French voyageurs used to transport passengers and cargo. Lewis bought two along the OHIO RIVER. They were called only "the white" and "the red" in the journals. The 39-foot-long white pirogue, commanded by

pirogue
BOB EVERTON

Richard WARFINGTON, seated 12 men, and the 42'-57long red pirogue, manned by hired French boatmen, seated 14 and carried nine tons. The Corps stored them by sinking them in water and covering them with branches before crossing the ROCKY MOUNTAINS in 1805. The red pirogue couldn't be used when it was retrieved, but the white pirogue was all right.

Platte River Forms at North Platte, Nebraska, from the North Platte and the South Platte, which both rise in the ROCKY MOUNTAINS of Colorado (with the North Platte detouring through Wyoming). The main Platte flows into the Missouri River at today's Plattsmouth, Nebraska, south of Omaha. French voyageurs opened fur trading here in the early 1700s, and the MOUTH of the Platte was a well known Missouri River landmark before the Corps of Discovery reached it on July 21, 1804. One of the men (either LABICHE or CRUZATTE, who both had Omaha Indian mothers and French fathers) previously had spent two winters trading on the Platte. Famously called "a mile wide and an inch deep," the Platte was six feet deep and 600 yards wide at its mouth when Clark noted that it "Cannot be navagated with Boats or Perogues."

poling When the river was too low for the KEELBOAT to be paddled, and the banks had no flat space for the men to CORDELLE it, the men poled the boat. Bracing against long, iron-tipped wooden poles that they planted on the river bottom, the men walked in single file toward the back of the boat, pushing the deck with their feet to make it go forward. One by one, they jumped aside and ran forward to begin again.

Pompeys Pillar Sandstone butte beside the YELLOW-STONE RIVER that rises 150' from its two-acre base. Today it is protected as Pompeys Pillar National Monument, northeast of Billings, Montana. Clark carved his name and the date here on July 25, 1806, which can still be seen.

Clark named it Pompy's Tower, using the nickname he had given SACAGAWEA'S son, Jean Baptiste CHARBONNEAU. Several theories exist to explain the nickname, but no one knows its origins. In writing his 1814 history of the expedition, Nicholas BIDDLE changed the name to Pompey's Pillar, which he thought more elegant. Today's geographical naming uses no apostrophes.

Pompy See CHARBONNEAU, JEAN BAPTISTE.

Pompeys Pillar
LARRY MAYER

portable soup

portable soup A rich broth of meat and vegetables cooked down to concentrate, then cooled, and stored as thick paste, cubes, or powder. The men mixed it into boiling water. The expedition started out with 193 pounds of it in lead cans. Containing no preservatives, the soup eventually grew rancid—but was eaten for nourishment anyway when food was scarce, especially in the 1805 BITTERROOT MOUNTAINS crossing.

portage Both the act of hiking around an obstacle in a river, and what such a place is called. The word comes from voyageurs, from the French word for "carry." When portaging, the men carried the freight overland, and sometimes the boats as well; sometimes the boats were guided over falls by ropes or even on logs. At the GREAT FALLS OF THE MISSOURI, a series of five waterfalls meant quite a long portage. There, the men built simple frames with slices of cottonwood trees for wheels, put the canoes loaded with freight on them, and hiked about eighteen miles overland pushing or pulling the crude "wagons." When the wind was in the right direction, they even hoisted sails on the wagons.

Potts, John (1776-1808?) Private in Sgt. ORDWAY'S squad. Transferred to the expedition from the regular army.

poultice Bandage moistened with medication, then used to cover a wound or an infected part of the body.

powderhorn Each man carried a powderhorn, often made of an animal horn, with the narrow end used for pouring powder into his GUN'S pan.

Lewis had the expedition's gunpowder supply sealed in lead canisters. When one was opened, its powder was distributed, then each man was responsible for keeping his powder dry and usable in his powderhorn. The canisters were melted and the lead poured into bullet molds.

prairie Open grassland with few or no trees. In the center of North America, prairie extends from Manitoba, Saskatchewan, and Alberta south into northern Mexico, and from western Indiana to the Rocky Mountain foothills. The wetter, eastern portion is tallgrass prairie, the central Great Plains is mixed-grass prairie, and the dry, western portion is shortgrass prairie. Tallgrass supports big bluestem, Indiangrass, and switchgrass that can reach 8' high. Shortgrass prairie holds blue grama, buffalograss, and sideoats grama. The captains learned that Indians set fire to the prairie as a signal to meet, so they did it also.

prairie dog (*Cynomys ludovicianus*) Mammal, about a foot long, with a 3"-4" tail, weighing only a few pounds. A group of

powder horn and powder bag hang from flintlock rifle
ROBERT F. MORGAN

prairie dog
DONALD M. JONES

many families creates underground burrows called a "town," where they go for safety and also to spend the winter sleeping. The first time they saw a prairie dog town, the captains poked a stick down one of its many entrances, but couldn't reach the bottom. They also poured five barrels of water into the hole, which never filled up.

prairie wolf The captains' term for the COYOTE.

prickly pear (*Opuntia polyacantha*) Low-lying cactus with long spines, a painful nuisance for the Corps over many miles. On July 19, 1805, near present Helena, Montana, Clark wrote that his feet were "constantly Stuck full [of] Prickley pear thorns, I puled out 17 by the light of the fire to night." When the cactus's bright yellow flowers were in bloom on July 15, 1805, Lewis called the plants "one of the beauties as well as the greatest pests of the plains."

prickly pear
BOB EVERTON

pronghorn (*Antilocapra americana*) Clark called it "the goat of this country," and today many people incorrectly call it an antelope. This mammal is built for short bursts of very high-speed running (up to 40 miles per hour) to escape predators. Both males and females have horns. Pronghorns live only in North America, in arid lands from western Mexico to southern Canada.

pronghorn
DONALD M. JONES

Pryor, Nathaniel Hale

Pryor, Nathaniel Hale (1772-1831) Sergeant who enlisted with Clark at Clarksville in 1803 along with his cousin Charles FLOYD. On the 1806 return, he went with Clark to the YELLOWSTONE RIVER and then led a party of SHANNON, HALL, and WINDSOR, to drive fifty horses to the MANDAN AND HIDATSA villages and then north to Canada. They were to trade the horses for supplies, and deliver a letter from the captains asking British trader Hugh Heney to persuade SIOUX INDIANS to visit Washington, D.C. Pryor's group left on July 24, upstream from today's Billings, Montana. Only two nights out, near today's Hardin on the Crow Indian Reservation, they camped at a creek swollen by a flash flood. Overnight, the horses were stolen. Pryor and his men tracked them for five miles on foot before giving up. They took their baggage and headed northeast, knowing they would meet the Yellowstone River. There they built two BULLBOATS and began floating toward the Missouri, to meet up with the Corps or go all the way to ST. LOUIS. On August 8, they reached Clark's party. That night, a WOLF bit Pryor's hand while he slept.

Continuing in the army after the expedition, Pryor was promoted to ensign (second lieutenant) and put in charge of the 1807 party that tried to return Chief SHEHEKE home after his visit to Washington, D.C. The group of Sheheke's and Rene JUSSEAUME's families, 14 soldiers and an interpreter, and 22 traders was attacked by 650 Arikara and Sioux Indians, who killed four traders and wounded six, injured three soldiers, including George SHANNON, and severely wounded JUSSEAUME. After

rattlesnake
BOB EVERTON

returning to St. Louis, Pryor offered to take SHEHEKE and his family on a safer but longer overland path, but the chief refused to leave without Jusseaume.

quadrant *See* SEXTANT.

quawmash The captains' spelling for camas. *See* ROOT VEGETABLES.

Quawmash Flats *See* WEIPPE PRAIRIE.

rat, pack (*Neotoma cinerea*) Bushy-tailed woodrat. Lewis wrote the first scientific description of this large rat on July 2, 1805, at the GREAT FALLS OF THE MISSOURI. He believed they ate PRICKLY PEAR cactus because he found cactus "hulls" plentiful around their nests in the river bluffs.

Rattlesnake Cliffs Named by Lewis for their plentiful inhabitants on August 10, 1805, the cliffs today are on public land southwest of Dillon, Montana.

rawhide Untanned animal hide that can be shaped, cut, or tied when wet, then shrinks and hardens upon drying. For quick repairs, it was the "duct tape" of the wilderness.

Reed, Moses (dates unknown) Originally a private in Sgt. FLOYD's squad, he deserted on August 4, 1804, saying he had left his knife at the previous night's camp. When he had not returned by the 7th, the captains sent DROUILLARD, Reubin FIELD, BRATTON, and LABICHE to bring him back, "dead or alive." Reed was captured and returned to the main party, COURT MARTIALLED on August 18, and sentenced to run the gantlet four times and be dishonorably discharged. He spent the winter at FORT MANDAN and was sent to ST. LOUIS with the RETURN PARTY in spring 1805.

return party Men who were designated to spend the first winter of 1804-1805 at FORT MANDAN and then return to ST. LOUIS with the KEELBOAT. When the return party, commanded by Cpl. Richard WARFINGTON, reached St. Louis on May 20, 1805, it was the first news of the expedition in a year. They carried journals and maps the captains had created during the first part of the trip, 67 mineral and 60 plant specimens, and specimens of 16 animal species that Lewis had preserved. Lewis also sent a live sharp-tailed GROUSE, and several live MAGPIES and PRAIRIE DOGS. The specimens went to President JEFFERSON via the Mississippi River and around the Atlantic coast to Baltimore, then overland to Washington, D.C. Of the living animals, one prairie dog survived.

Ricaras or **Ricarees** The captains' names for ARIKARA Indians.

Robertson, John (ca. 1780-?) Possibly named John Robinson, he may have transferred to the expedition from the army artillery. On April 1, 1804, he was designated for the RETURN PARTY, but his name was not on the list of squad assignments on May 26. WHITEHOUSE'S journal, on June 21, 1804, tells that an artilleryman from the Corps was sent back down the Missouri that day but does not name him. And then Robertson's name disappears from the record.

Rocky Mountains The captains expected the Rockies to be a single range of mountains between the highest sources of the MISSOURI RIVER and those of the COLUMBIA RIVER, where they could PORTAGE canoes across. Instead, the Rocky Mountains include several main ranges, and within those are row after row of peaks. The major Rockies ranges the expedition crossed, from east to west, are: Tobacco Root Mountains, Beaverhead Mountains, BITTERROOT RANGE, and Clearwater Mountains.

rod Surveyor's linear measurement equal to 5.5 yards.

Rooster Rock After portaging the CASCADES OF THE COLUMBIA on November 2, 1805, the Corps camped near this landmark in today's Rooster Rock State Park, east of Portland, Oregon. Passing it again on April 6, 1806, the captains still left the rock unnamed.

root vegetables Both nomadic and sedentary Indian nations used starchy root vegetables to eat raw or cooked and to dry and preserve. The Corps ate any type they were introduced to, primarily:
bitterroot (Lewisia rediviva) Rare today, this was a staple of Rocky Mountain Indian diets. Roots were harvested in spring before the flowers appeared, the bitter black skin scraped off, and inner white part boiled. After cooking they were dried and ground into powder, making a starch that thickened soups. Lewis described the plant scientifically on August 22, 1805,

root vegetables

breadroot
COURTESY OF LARKSPUR BOOKS/A. SCOTT EARLE

wapato
COURTESY OF LARKSPUR BOOKS/A. SCOTT EARLE

at CAMP FORTUNATE. He found the taste "nauseous." Botanist Frederick Pursh later named the plant for Lewis, who took specimens home.

breadroot (Psoralea esculenta Pursh) Small tubers with notable sugar content. Eaten raw, roasted, and in stew, or dried and ground into flour. Lewis likened the taste to hominy (*see* CORN). He first mentioned them at CALUMET BLUFF campsite near today's Crofton, Nebraska, as the "ground potato" that was substituted for bread, and wrote his scientific description on May 8, 1805, east of today's Fort Peck DAM, Montana, adding that breadroot seemed to be healthful and moderately nutritious but had an "insipid" taste.

camas (Camassia quamash) The small (up to 1" diameter) bulb of this blue-flowered plant is onionlike. To preserve them, Indians cooked them by burying with heated rocks in a pit covered with dirt, then sun-dried them or pounded them into flour for bread. They also could be eaten raw or boiled in soup. The Corps often cooked them with parched CORN. The captains called WEIPPE PRAIRIE, Idaho, "Quamash Flats" because it was a major camas-gathering site. The camas was blooming there on June 11, 1806, when Lewis wrote his scientific description.

cous (Lomatium cous) Often written "cows" in the journals, this is also called biscuit-root. The raw root tastes like celery, but Indians usually

dried and ground the root to make a flat bread. The Corps liked boiling them with onion into a "mush." Lewis first mentioned cous on November 1, 1805, when the Corps camped up the COLUMBIA RIVER from today's Bonneville DAM.

wapato (Sagittaria latifolia) Arrowhead. A plant that grows in marshes or slow-moving waters. Indian women of the COLUMBIA RIVER Valley harvested them by wading barefoot in chest-deep water beside a small canoe and loosening the roots with their toes. When the roots floated to the surface, they were put into the boat. Wapato was used like potato, and also dried and ground into flour. Lewis lagged behind the Corps at CELILO FALLS on October 22, 1805, to watch the root being harvested. It was a diet mainstay during the winter at FORT CLATSOP.

yampah (Perideridia gairdneri) Gairdner's yampah. Harvested in the fall, this parsnip-like, mildly anise-flavored root is easy to digest. It was eaten raw, boiled, or dried then pounded into flour. Lewis first described it for science on August 26, 1805, as SHOSHONE women dug them up en route over LEMHI PASS. He did not collect a specimen.

camas
COURTESY OF LARKSPUR BOOKS/A. SCOTT EARLE

Ruptáre Farther Mandan village from FORT MANDAN, across the Missouri River from the MOUTH of the Knife River. BLACK CAT was its chief, and was a good friend to Lewis and Clark and other white traders who visited. *See also* MANDAN AND HIDATSA INDIANS.

Benjamin Rush

Rush, Benjamin (1745-1813) A prominent Philadelphia physician and friend of Thomas JEFFERSON, who gave Lewis a basic course in medicines and techniques in 1803. Rush favored BLEEDING and various methods of purging the body, acceptable practice at the time. He also helped create the list of cultural questions to be asked of Indian nations about their beliefs and customs.

Rush's pills A strong laxative pill that Benjamin RUSH created with jalap and calomel. Lewis purchased 50 dozen of them for the trip.

Sacagawea (ca. 1788-1812?) She was a Lemhi SHOSHONE woman of about seventeen in 1804, who had been captured by the HIDATSAS five years previously. She and her husband, Toussaint CHARBONNEAU, were hired as interpreters early in 1805, once the captains understood that they would need to obtain horses to cross the ROCKY MOUNTAINS, and that the likely source would be the Shoshones. Her first child, Jean Baptiste CHARBONNEAU, was born shortly before the Corps left FORT MANDAN, and she carried him along to the Pacific and back. She probably died around 1812 at Fort Manuel Lisa near future Mobridge, South Dakota.

As the captains wrote her name, the "g" is pronounced hard, *Suh-*COG*-uh-wee-uh*. No one knows whether that was her Shoshone name. Another commonly used spelling has been Sacajawea. If the name came from the Hidatsa language of her captors, a better spelling would be *Sakakawea*. The latter is used throughout North Dakota, home of the Hidatsas.

Sacs The captains' name for Sauk Indians.

Detail from the Eugene Daub sculpture of Sacagawea, Kansas City, Missouri
J. AGEE

St. Louis, Missouri At the MOUTH of the MISSOURI RIVER on the Mississippi River. In 1803, St. Louis was a village of about 1,000 to 1,400 residents including slaves and freemen. It was the capital of Upper Louisiana (*see* LOUISIANA PURCHASE), administered by Frenchmen on behalf of Spain. *See also* CAMP DUBOIS.

Salish Indians The Corps of Discovery met the Salish Indians, allies of the SHOSHONES, in Ross's Hole, near future Sula, Montana, on September 4, 1805, and spent two days with them. The Salish, seeing their first white people, "recvd us friendly," Clark wrote. The captains mistakenly called the people "Flatheads," although they did not practice head-flattening, and today the Confederated Salish and Kootenai Tribes live on the Flathead Reservation in northwest Montana.

salmon Fish that was a mainstay of Indian diets west of the CONTINENTAL DIVIDE, and of the Corps over winter 1805-1806. Salmon can be anadromous (born in fresh water, spend adulthood in salt water, but return to fresh water to lay and fertilize eggs). Some species spawn in the spring, some in autumn. Some species die after spawning.

In the fall of 1805 and again in the spring of 1806, the Corps of Discovery witnessed salmon runs on the COLUMBIA RIVER.

salmon
BOB EVERTON

Indians of many nations gathered along the banks to harvest and preserve salmon. The captains thought the fish were dying from disease, and refused to eat them. Instead, they insisted on buying pounded salmon (see below).

chinook (Oncorhynchus tshawytscha) King salmon, the largest Pacific salmon at 2'–5' long. Lewis called this the "common salmon" during the winter of 1805-1806.

coho (Oncorhynchus kisutch) Silver salmon, 17"-38" long. Spawns in autumn.

sockeye (Oncorhynchus nerka) Red salmon, 20"-28" long. Born in fresh water, it may spend a few months or as many as two years there before going downstream to the ocean. It spawns in autumn, so the Corps saw it running up the Columbia as they approached the Pacific in 1805.

salmonberry *See* BERRIES.

salmon, pounded The term for dried SALMON that Columbia River natives pounded fine between two stones, then stored in baskets lined with stretched and dried salmon skins. The tribal name of the CLATSOP INDIANS refers to pounded salmon.

At CELILO FALLS, Clark wrote admiringly of how they "neetly preserved" the fish. Seven 90- to 100-pound filled baskets were put close together, with five more stacked on top, and the whole group was wrapped in woven mats and tied tightly together. Clark was told the salmon inside stayed "Sound and Sweet Several years." The food was an important trade item to area Indians and to "the whites [sic] people who visit the mouth of this river."

Salmon River Although the NEZ PERCE said this was impassable for canoes, Clark took the guide TOBY, and three Corps members, to see for himself. Leaving CAMEAHWAIT'S village on August 20, 1805, they went down the Lemhi River to the Salmon, and continued west from today's North Fork, Idaho, down the Salmon. On the 23rd, Clark gave up when he came to rocky cliffs that surrounded river rapids. Horses could not get to the water there, and the canoes would have to be let down on ropes. The Nez Perce had been right.

salmon trout On March 12, 1806, Lewis described two species of what he called "salmon trout," both new to science: *steelhead* (which is a TROUT), and *coho* (which is a SALMON).

salt pork Fat from the pork belly, cured in salt without smoking. It needed to be soaked in fresh water before it was usable. Salt pork, which has less meat than bacon, was boiled or fried. The Corps made their supply last—and had tastier meals—by eating fresh game as often as possible.

sandbar A river "island" of loose sand constantly moved and reshaped by the current. In the days before DAMS, the Missouri River was filled with them, making the men tow or lift the boats around or across. On September 21, 1804, at 1:30 in the morning, the guard yelled to waken the men. They had camped in the BIG BEND OF THE MISSOURI on a sandbar now dissolving right under them.

Scannon *See* SEAMAN.

Schuylkill Arsenal (*pronounced* SKOO-*kle*) Established in 1800 in PHILADELPHIA to store ammunition and army supplies. The arsenal also was a center for military clothing and flags hand-stitched by area women and men, who obtained cut pieces here and worked at home. Beginning in 1818, the arsenal was dedicated to supplying clothing and cloth items, serving through the War of 1812 and the Civil War.

Supplies from the arsenal were part of the 3,500 pounds of goods that Lewis assembled in Philadelphia in the summer of 1803.

scurvy Disease caused by lack of Vitamin C in the diet, which harms connective tissues, cartilage, and bones. It causes easy bruising, bleeding gums and joints, and can cause anemia. The Corps of Discovery did not eat a balanced diet, but David J. Peck, D.O., argues that they probably did not develop scurvy because they obtained some Vitamin C from animal kidneys and livers, and also from fish during the winter of 1805-1806.

seal, harbor (*Phoca vitulina richardii*) The captains mistook this new-to-science species for the SEA OTTER on November 3, 1805, but by February 23, 1806,

harbor seals
DONALD M. JONES

understood that it was a different species. The Corps saw them as far up the COLUMBIA RIVER as the CASCADES OF THE COLUMBIA. Their range is north of the Equator, in near-shore water, and they haul themselves out onto mudflats and SANDBARS. They are five to six feet in length, and males can weigh 300 pounds.

Seaman The Newfoundland dog that Lewis purchased in 1803, sometime between leaving Washington, D.C., in April and leaving Pittsburgh at the end of August that year. These large (100-150 pounds) working dogs have thick, curly coats for warmth, and webbed feet for swimming. They were used along the New England and Canadian coast of the Atlantic Ocean to rescue sailors, or "seamen," from shipwrecks. For many years, historians thought Lewis called the dog "Scannon," but now have decided that was an early misreading of the captains' handwriting.

Seaman
BOB EVERTON

serviceberry See BERRIES.

sextant Used by surveyors and sailors to determine latitude, in the Corps' case how far north of the Equator they were. One component is the arc (curved segment) of an imaginary perfect circle, marked off in 60 degrees. A moveable arm pivoting on the center of the imaginary circle equals the circle's radius (half its diameter). A mirror is mounted on this arm. A nonmoveable telescope is attached to the frame.

sextant
BOB EVERTON

When Clark pointed the telescope at the horizon, he could see both the horizon and the mirror's reflection of a star, usually the North Star (Polaris, above the North Pole), or the sun at exact noon. (The captains depended on their journals for keeping track of the date, and the CHRONOMETER for precise time.) He then carefully moved the radial arm until the mirror image of the star seemed to be sitting on the natural horizon, if it could be seen, or on the ARTIFICIAL HORIZON. From the sextant's arc, he read the number of degrees between the star and the horizon. Considering the date and exact time, he then used tables published for sailors, and obtained the latitude. Earlier forms of the sextant (whose arc equals one sixth of a circle) had been the quadrant (one fourth of a circle, or 90°) in the mid-1500s, followed by the octant (one eighth of a circle, or 45°) in the latter 1600s. Besides their sextant, the captains carried an octant, which they confusingly called a "Hadley's quadrant." George Hadley (1685-1768), the English physicist who described how Earth's air circulates, wrote about quadrant use, and a published 1825 list of surveyor's instruments used by sailors includes "the astronomical Quadrant and Hadley's Octant, or Sextant."

See also LATITUDE, LONGITUDE.

Shannon, George (1785-1836) Private in Sgt. PRYOR'S squad, and the Corps' youngest enlisted man, born in 1785. He probably enlisted with Lewis on the OHIO RIVER in 1803. In August 1804, in future South Dakota, he was lost from the corps for sixteen days, the longest any man was separated. Rushing to catch up, he was actually ahead of them. During that time, he had only one rabbit and wild grapes to eat. Finally, he sat down on the bank of the Missouri hoping to meet a trading boat going downstream, and the Corps caught up with him. His hunting skills improved greatly during the expedition. Shannon was in Nathaniel PRYOR'S ill-fated horse party in 1806. In 1807, in Pryor's party trying to escort Chief SHEHEKE home, he lost a leg as a result of battle with ARIKARAS. *See also* CANOES.

sheep, bighorn (*Ovis canadensis*) Horned sheep living from the ROCKY MOUNTAINS into Death Valley, they reach 3.5 feet in height at the shoulder and 275 pounds (males). The males' horns grow into coils on either side of the head. The captains first heard of them on October 1, 1804, from Jean Vallé at his trading post

north of the Cheyenne River's MOUTH in today's South Dakota. Vallé had seen bighorns in the Black Hills. Joseph FIELD saw the first living specimens of "the big horn animal" on April 26, 1805, when sent up the YELLOWSTONE RIVER for a short exploration. The Corps continued to see bighorns on the plains around the Upper Missouri, and Clark and BRATTON each shot a specimen on May 25, 1805. The animal already was known to science, having been collected in Canada. The Corps may also have seen Audubon bighorn sheep, a slightly smaller subspecics that now is extinct.

bighorn sheep
DONALD M. JONES

Sheheke

Sheheke Mandan chief of MITUTANKA. He, his wife and son, went to Washington, D.C., with the Corps in 1806, to meet JEFFERSON and see the United States. Because of Plains Indians wars, American soldiers needed two tries to escort him home. Nathaniel PRYOR led an 1807 party that suffered bloody losses (*see also* SHANNON) before turning back to St. Louis, where Sheheke and his family, with the JUSSEAUME family, waited sixteen months for Gov. Meriwether Lewis to organize a larger escort combining military men and civilians. This second escort succeeded in getting Sheheke home in September 1809, after a journey of more than three months. Sadly for the chief, his descriptions of whites' cities and culture were so illogical to the MANDANS that they rejected them as tall tales, and his status declined.

Shields, John (1769-1809) Private in Sgt. PRYOR'S squad who enlisted with Clark at Clarksville in 1803. He was the Corps's oldest Army member. At CAMP DUBOIS, he was mutinous toward Sgt. ORDWAY in the captains' absence, but had no more discipline problems. His work as the Corps' gunsmith received the captains' great praise as he repaired the irreplaceable items time and again. He also did blacksmithing and carpentry. At FORT MANDAN, he earned corn for the expedition by making metal battle axes to the Indians' specifications. Although Lewis asked that Shields receive extra rewards for his contributions, Congress authorized only the standard private's pay.

Short Narrows See THE DALLES.

Shoshone Indians SACAGAWEA'S people, the Lemhi Shoshones, were part of the Northern Shoshones. Their home country was the SNAKE RIVER area of future Idaho. The Rockies were their protection from Indian nations better armed than they were. They traveled over the mountains once a year to hunt BISON around the THREE FORKS OF THE MISSOURI, which is where Sacagawea was captured by the Hidatsa Indians (*see* MANDAN AND HIDATSA INDIANS).

At FORT MANDAN, the captains learned enough about the mysterious ROCKY MOUNTAINS to understand that they would need horses to carry their baggage over them. When they learned that the Shoshones lived there, the captains were determined to trade with them. Relations between the Shoshones, who had never met whites before, and the Corps were very cordial.

From 1875 to 1906, the Northern Shoshones shared a small reservation in the Lemhi Valley near Tendoy, Idaho, with the Bannock and Sheepeater Indians. When the reservation was closed, many of the Shoshones moved to Fort Hall Indian Reservation in eastern Idaho, but some chose to stay in the Tendoy area. *See also* CAMEAHWAIT, CAMP FORTUNATE, TOBY.

Sioux Indians Powerful nation of nomadic BISON-hunters of the northern Great Plains. The Corps met with two groups of Sioux Indians, the Yankton (now Dakota) and the Teton (later divided into the Brulé, Hunkpapa, Miniconjou, Oglala, Sans Arc, Two Kettle, and Blackfeet Sioux). The Yanktons and the Tetons spent time along the MISSOURI RIVER and were trading with whites regularly by 1804.

The *Yanktons* were met in friendly council at the CALUMET BLUFF, down-

A Dakota man in the process of signing "white man"

stream from today's Gavins Point DAM, held from August 30 through September 1, 1804. The Corps camped on the Missouri's future Nebraska side, and the Yanktons on the South Dakota side. Today they live on the Lower Brulé Indian Reservation, southeast of Pierre, South Dakota, and the Yankton Indian Reservation west of Yankton, South Dakota.

The *Tetons* met in council with the Corps September 25-28, 1804, around the site of today's Pierre, South Dakota. They were hospitable but on edge, finding it odd that white men came with many TRADE GOODS but wanted to save so much of their supply. Communications were hampered by poor interpretation; the Corps had no Sioux speaker, so CRUZATTE spoke his native Omaha to Omaha captives among the Tetons. Misunderstandings were taken as preludes to warfare by both sides, but were settled without fighting. Still, on the return trip in 1806, the Corps refused to visit again with the Tetons. Today the Teton Sioux live on the Cheyenne River, Crow Creek, Lower Brulé, Pine Ridge, and Rosebud Indian reservations.

Skillute Indians The captains' name for Watlala Indians.

Snake Indians The captains' name for SHOSHONE INDIANS.

Snake River Principal tributary of the COLUMBIA RIVER, flowing into it northwest of Walla Walla, Washington. The Corps traveled downstream from the MOUTH of the CLEARWATER RIVER on the Snake (near Lewiston, Idaho, and Clarkston, Washington) to reach the Columbia. They were on the Snake October 10-16, 1805.

snowblindness Painful burn of the cornea (clear part of the eye over the lens) by ultraviolet rays reflected from bright surfaces. The cornea heals itself quickly, so easing the pain is the main medical treatment. The captains carried soothing eye drops of lead acetate and zinc sulfate, but learned another treatment from the Mandans. They threw snow on heated rocks and let the steam soothe the eyes.

soup *See* PORTABLE SOUP.

Spirit Mound North of future Vermillion, South Dakota, the captains heard about this hill that local people thought was home to 18"-tall devils with large heads, who used very sharp, long-flying arrows to kill any humans who came near. They of course went to look, on August 25, 1804. Today on private land, Spirit Mound can be viewed from a turnout on South Dakota Route 19.

spy The captains used the word to mean someone who scouted ahead, or the process of scouting.

spyglass Small, collapsible telescope.

spyglass
J. AGEE

starboard The right-hand side of a boat as one faces forward in it. At the time, also referred to the right side of a river as one faces downstream, but Clark used the term simply to mean the right side of the river from his position.

sun glass A glass lens used to concentrate sun rays onto tinder for fire-starting. Some were included in the captains' TRADE GOODS.

tanning Turning animal hides into leather for preservation. Steps include scraping off all membrane on the flesh side (call "fleshing"), cutting off long hair, shaving off shorter hairs, and treating the hide with chemicals. Indians used the animal's brain as a chemical in tanning, which produces a soft, odorless leather.

tern, least (*Sterna antillarum*) Water bird that dives for prey but does not swim. The least tern, which Lewis first described on August 5, 1804, on the Iowa-Nebraska section of the Missouri, is only 9" long. He incorrectly thought they lived there year-round; they migrate south for winter.

The Dalles Two-part obstruction of the COLUMBIA RIVER at the upstream (east) end of the COLUMBIA RIVER GORGE. Going downstream on October 24, 1805, the

Part of The Dalles of the Columbia River, these rock formations now are under the waters of Lake Celilo
REPRODUCED FROM THE COLLECTIONS OF THE LIBRARY OF CONGRESS

Corps reached the *Short Narrows*, where rocks squeezed the river to only 45 yards wide for a distance of a quarter mile. Beyond that was the *Long Narrows*, 200 yards wide but five miles long. To Clark, "the water was agitated in a most Shocking manner…" through The Dalles.

The Corps' non-swimmers carried the baggage around by land on the Washington side. Others were assigned to stand by with rope, ready to throw it to dumped canoeists. Then the canoes came through, the first and second smoothly, the third taking on water but paddled to shore, and the fourth with no trouble.

With CELILO FALLS, The Dalles marked a major division in Native American cultures. Clark was welcomed into a lodge here, among "the first wooden houses in which Indians have lived Since we left…the ILLINOIS…" At this place also, Indian languages changed from those of the family that included NEZ PERCE to those of the family including coastal languages. The Nez Perce chiefs Twisted Hair and Tetoharsky, who had traveled with the Corps introducing them, made ready to return home because they could no longer speak to residents, who were also their enemies.

Today, water raised by The Dalles DAM covers this one-time Columbia River landmark that is upstream from The Dalles, Oregon.

A replica Chinook longhouse at Fort Stevens State Park, Oregon, shows the homes of lower Columbia River people who traded with the expedition
GEORGE WUERTHNER

thimbleberry *See* BERRIES.

Thompson, John B. (dates unknown) Private in Sgt. FLOYD'S squad. Possibly a surveyor.

Three Forks of the Missouri River The HEADWATERS where the Gallatin, Madison, and Jefferson rivers join to form the MISSOURI RIVER in southwestern Montana. The Corps was assigned to locate them. Clark's advance party (seeking SHOSHONE INDIANS) arrived on July 25, 1805, and Lewis with the main party arrived on the 27th. The captains named them for Albert Gallatin (then Secretary of the Treasury), James Madison (Secretary of State and future president), and President Thomas JEFFERSON.

Thwaites, Reuben Gold (1853-1913) Edited and prepared the first edition of Lewis and Clark's expedition journals, published in 1901. He excluded GASS'S journal, which had been published separately, but found and included FLOYD'S and WHITEHOUSE'S.

tippet A ceremonial collar. Lewis obtained one made of ermine tails from CAMEAHWAIT, and wore it with his leather clothing (*at right*) to pose for a painter back home.

Lewis, by Charles B. J. F. Saint-Memin, 1807
ACC. NO. 1971-125, COLLECTION OF THE NEW-YORK HISTORICAL SOCIETY

Toby Swooping Eagle, a NEZ PERCE guide, is called "Old Toby" the only time his name is mentioned in the journals. Probably "old" to distinguish him from his son, who joined him. The nickname may come from the SHOSHONE for "he furnished the white man brains." Toby first guided Clark's reconnaissance of the SALMON RIVER (August 20-26, 1805). Then he was hired to lead the Corps to and across the LOLO TRAIL through the BITTERROOT MOUNTAINS, and he and his son traveled with them until October 9. They left suddenly without collecting their pay.

tomahawk All the men carried army-issued tomahawks, a useful tool and weapon. At one end it had an ax blade and a pipe bowl, at the other the mouthpiece of the pipe. It could be used as a hammer as well as an ax.

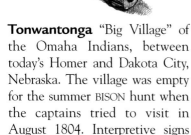

tomahawk
BOB EVERTON

Tonwantonga "Big Village" of the Omaha Indians, between today's Homer and Dakota City, Nebraska. The village was empty for the summer BISON hunt when the captains tried to visit in August 1804. Interpretive signs now tell the site's story.

trade goods Small, easily carried items—most made of glass or metal—valuable to Indians who did not have the technology for making them. In the Corps' supply were BEADS, 4,600 sewing needles, 14 pounds of knitting needles, 15 dozen scissors, 288 thimbles, ribbon, 2,800 fish hooks, 13 pounds of handkerchiefs, 48 "Callico ruffled" shirts, 1,152 moccasin awls, 15 dozen polished-pewter mirrors, 63 pounds of tobacco, and 8 dozen SUN GLASSES. They were given as presents and also bartered for food.

trade goods
J. AGEE

Travelers' Rest Campsite, named by the captains, near today's Lolo, Montana, where the Corps stayed September 9–11, 1805, just before their main ROCKY MOUNTAINS crossing, and rested on the return trip June 30 to July 3, 1806. The site opened to the public as a Montana State Park in 2002.

trencher Sturdy, wooden, all-purpose dish used in frontier homes and carried by soldiers. Its shallow indentation could hold soup as well as solid food.

trencher
J. AGEE

trout Fish in the SALMON family. They can be anadromous (born in fresh water, spend adulthood in salt water, but return to fresh water to lay and fertilize eggs), or landlocked.

brook (Salvelinus fontinalis) Known to science and familiar to Lewis from home. He used it as a comparative to describe the cutthroat trout.

cutthroat (Oncorhynchus clarki) Has both anadromous and landlocked forms. Spawns in February and March. GOODRICH caught half a dozen at the GREAT FALLS OF THE MISSOURI on June 13, 1805, when he was part of Lewis's advance party. Lewis wrote the first scientific description, before enjoying a meal including the "fine trout."

rainbow (Salmo gairdneri) A landlocked steelhead that has adapted to living only in fresh water.

steelhead (Oncorhynchus mykiss) To Lewis, it was a species of "SALMON TROUT." Steelheads do not die after spawning the first time.

tumors The captains' term for boils, abscesses, or other swollen skin infections.

Tuttle, Ebenezer (1773-?) Private in the RETURN PARTY. Transferred to the expedition from the army artillery.

ulcer The captains use this to mean an open sore on the skin.

United States The nation was twenty-eight years old when the expedition started up the Missouri in 1804. In 1803 the 17th state (Ohio) had joined the union, and no more entered until Louisiana in 1812. The U.S. flag design was not altered as promptly as later on, so the expedition's flags had 15 stars and 15 stripes.

The captains sometimes used the abbreviation "U' States," as did Union soldiers six decades later, during the Civil War.

Upper Portage Camp Upstream from the GREAT FALLS OF THE MISSOURI, at today's White Bear Islands.

Vancouver, George (1757-1798) British naval captain who explored the northwestern coast of North America in 1792. He sent his lieutenant, William Broughton, as far upstream on the COLUMBIA RIVER as today's Reed Island, east of Portland, Oregon.

Meriwether Lewis carried copies of Vancouver's maps, and so knew what to expect downstream from Reed Island.

Walla Walla Indians Living in the area where today's Walla Walla River flows into the COLUMBIA RIVER, the nation was first met on October 18, 1805. As invited by Chief YELLEPPIT, the Corps visited longer on the return trip, April 27-30, 1806. After leaving them then, Lewis thought the Walla Wallas "the most hospitable, honest, and sincere people that we have met in our voyage." Forty-nine years later they moved onto the Umatilla Indian Reservation in Oregon, with the Cayuse and the Umatillas.

wapato See ROOT VEGETABLES.

Warfington, Richard (1777-?) Corporal in charge of the RETURN PARTY. His army enlistment expired in August 1804, but he agreed to stay with the Corps until the following spring in order to command the returning KEELBOAT.

Warner See WERNER, WILLIAM.

Flags weren't changed quickly in those days. All the expedition's flags held 15 stars like this replica, even though the U.S. had 17 states. J. AGEE

Weippe Prairie (*WEE-ipe*) Southeast of Orofino, Idaho, in the NEZ PERCE homeland. To the captains, it was "Quamash Flats," where the Nez Perce came annually to harvest their staple ROOT VEGETABLE, camas. Clark's advance party arrived here on September 20, 1806, coming down from the BITTERROOT MOUNTAINS, trailed by Lewis and the main party the next day.

On the homeward trip, the Corps reached Weippe Prairie and stayed June 10-15, 1806, before trying to cross the Bitterroots and finding the snow still too deep. They returned to Weippe Prairie, arriving June 21, and stayed until the 24th, when five Nez Perce young men agreed to guide them over the LOLO TRAIL.

Today Weippe Prairie is one of 38 sites in Nez Perce National Historical Park, which is headquartered at Spalding, Idaho.

Weiser, Peter M. (1781-?) Private in Sgt. PRYOR'S squad. Probably transferred to the expedition from the army infantry.

Werner, William (dates unknown) Private in Sgt. ORDWAY'S squad. Possibly transferred to the expedition from the regular army. He and Hugh HALL were COURT MARTIALLED on May 17, 1804, for being AWOL at St. Charles, Missouri, and sentenced to twenty-five lashes of the whip. The court recommended leniency and Clark did not carry out the punishment.

Lewis wrote that when camas bloomed, it looked like a lake of blue—just as shown here
COURTESY OF LARKSPUR BOOKS/A. SCOTT EARLE

White, Isaac

White, Isaac (ca. 1774-?) Private in the RETURN PARTY. Transferred to the expedition from the army artillery.

White Cliffs Going westward on the MISSOURI RIVER, the Corps of Discovery was passing through the MISSOURI BREAKS in central Montana on May 31, 1805. In the White Cliffs area, Lewis described the "romantic appearance" of the rock that looked like the ruins of elegant buildings, or columns complete with pedestals and capitals, rising 100' above the river. The rocks lining the river are sandstone with shale and shonkinite. Since the sandstone erodes more rapidly than the other rock types, shapes like ledges, ridges, and towers appear. The White Cliffs are much the same as when Lewis described them, and a limited number of canoeists and rafters are permitted on the river each summer.

Whitehouse, Joseph (ca. 1775-?) Private in Sgt. PRYOR'S squad. Transferred to the expedition from the army infantry. He was one of the privates who voluntarily kept a journal, which has been published. Whitehouse often stitched clothing for his companions. He served in the Army during the War of 1812, but Clark lost track of him after Whitehouse deserted in 1817.

white pudding *See* BOUDIN BLANC.

The White Cliffs today look much as they did when the expedition passed by MONTANA MAGAZINE

Willard
FROM *THE TRAIL OF LEWIS AND CLARK,* BY OLIN D. WHEELER (1904)

Willard, Alexander Hamilton (1778-1865) Private in ORDWAY'S squad. Transferred to the expedition from the army artillery, where he had been in charge of maintaining his company's arms and equipment. Court martialled on July 12, 1804, for sleeping on sentry duty, he was sentenced to 100 lashes of the whip, applied over four days. For the rest of that day, the captains halted travel at the MOUTH of the Big Nemaha River in today's Nebraska, to "rest the men who are much fatigued." Willard was one of the Corps' blacksmiths, and from his earlier army experience was able to assist SHIELDS in gun repair. *See also* CANOES.

Windsor, Richard (dates unknown) Private in Sgt. FLOYD'S squad. Transferred to the expedition from the army infantry. He was in Nathaniel PRYOR'S ill-fated horse party in 1806.

Wisdom River Today's Big Hole River, tributary to the JEFFERSON RIVER in Montana. The captains named it for one of Thomas JEFFERSON'S virtues.

Wishram-Wasco Indians Closely allied nations along the COLUMBIA RIVER, they were the easternmost of peoples who spoke Chinookan languages like those of the Pacific coast. The captains found the Wishrams living on the Columbia's north (future Washington) side and the Wascos living on the south (Oregon) side, downstream from CELILO FALLS. Today many of the Wishrams live on the Yakama Indian Reservation in Washington, and Wascos on Warm Springs Reservation, Oregon.

Meeting them on October 26, 1805, the captains misunderstood the tribal names. They believed the Wishrams called themselves "Echelute," which actually means "I am a Wishram Indian." They thought the Wascos called themselves "Che-luc-it-te-quar," which means "he is pointing at him"—what the captains must have been doing as they asked.

Wistar, Caspar (1761-1818) A friend of JEFFERSON and, like him, a man of wide interests. Wistar was a physician and headed the anatomy department of the future University of Pennsylvania in Philadelphia; he wrote the United States' first anatomy textbook. He was the nation's foremost fossils expert, and also interested in botany. In the summer of 1803, he helped train Lewis, teaching him about fossil finds and sharing his theory that mastodons might still roam the PRAIRIES.

wolf, gray (*Canis lupus*) Clark noted the first sighting of a now-extinct type of gray wolf (*Canis lupus nubilus*) on June 30, 1804, just after the Corps pushed off from the future site of Kansas City, Kansas. The following May 5, in future McCone County, Montana, Lewis described it in detail. He noted it was not as large as, and was heavier than, the wolf of the Atlantic states. This light-colored animal, called the "buffalo wolf" or "Great Plains wolf," was thought extinct by 1926, but scientists today believe descendants live in Upper Michigan, Minnesota, and Wisconsin.

Moving from the Missouri River system into the ROCKY MOUNTAINS, and then at FORT CLATSOP, the

Corps saw gray wolves (*Canis lupus*). On January 6, 1806, Clark reported that neighboring Indians used snares to catch wolves. During his MARIAS RIVER exploration, on July 14, 1806, Lewis counted twenty-seven wolves around a BISON carcass, while "wolves are in great numbers howling around us…"

Today gray wolves live in Canada and Alaska, but some have lightly recolonized a corridor east of the Rocky Mountains through Montana into Wyoming, after humans reintroduced them. They stand 26"-32" at the shoulder, with males measuring 5' to 6.5' from nose to tail and weighing 70 to 110 pounds.

Frost covers this gray wolf, but the animal's natural color ranges from nearly white to black DONALD M. JONES

Worthington, Wortheyton *See* WARFINGTON, RICHARD.

yampah *See* ROOT VEGETABLES.

Yelleppit Chief of the WALLA WALLA INDIAN village where the Corps stayed on October 18, 1805, near today's Walula, Washington. CRUZATTE played his fiddle, to the villagers' delight, and the chief asked the Corps to stay longer. They were eager to get to the Pacific Ocean, and promised a longer visit the following spring. They returned on April 27, 1806, and stayed to the 29th.

Hospitable Chief Yelleppit invited neighboring Yakamas, and Lewis estimated that 550 Indian men, women, and children sang and danced—for and with—the Corps on the 27th.

Better still, Chief Yelleppit described an overland shortcut the Corps could take to return to the CLEARWATER RIVER. Since they had mapped the SNAKE RIVER in 1805, they did not have to return by its waters, and could save at least eighty miles.

Yellowstone River A major tributary of the MISSOURI RIVER that flows from Yellowstone Lake in Yellowstone National Park, Wyoming, through Montana to meet the Missouri in western North Dakota. At 670 miles, it is the longest river with no DAM in the contiguous U.S.

Knowing from FORT MANDAN informants that they were nearing it, Lewis took four men and walked ahead on the chilly morning of April 25, 1805. He found the Yellowstone in a fertile valley covered with BISON, ELK, and PRONGHORNS. The main party arrived the next day.

The river seemed worth more exploration than the captains had time for in 1805. If the Yellowstone was navigable for a good distance, that was important to learn. Over winter at FORT CLATSOP they planned for Clark and part of the group, including SACAGAWEA, to go from CAMP FORTUNATE to the upper reaches of the Yellowstone, exploring downstream to the Missouri. There they would stop and wait for Lewis's group to arrive from exploring the MARIAS RIVER. Clark's party entered the Yellowstone's waters at the site of today's Livingston, Montana, on July 15, 1806, and reached the river's MOUTH on August 3, 1806.

York (ca. 1770-?) The African-American slave who belonged to and had grown up with Clark, and traveled as a civilian with the expedition. He shared in most duties, was an attentive nurse to the sick, and went out hunting alone with his own GUN. (It was illegal in slave states for slaves to travel alone or use guns.) He seems to have been a big man, because Clark wrote that on New Year's Day 1806,

when the men were dancing with Indians, the CLATSOPS were surprised at how light on his feet York was "for So large a man." According to Clark, York was amused that Indians thought he was a white man in black war paint, and let them examine his skin; he also teased youngsters by saying he used to be a cannibal, and small children were his favorite food. After Clark

Charles M. Russell's painting "York" imagines what the man looked like as Mandan people investigated whether he wore paint
COURTESY OF THE MONTANA HISTORICAL SOCIETY

finally freed his slave after 1811, York set up a wagon-freight business in Tennessee that eventually failed. He died of cholera en route to ST. LOUIS before 1832.

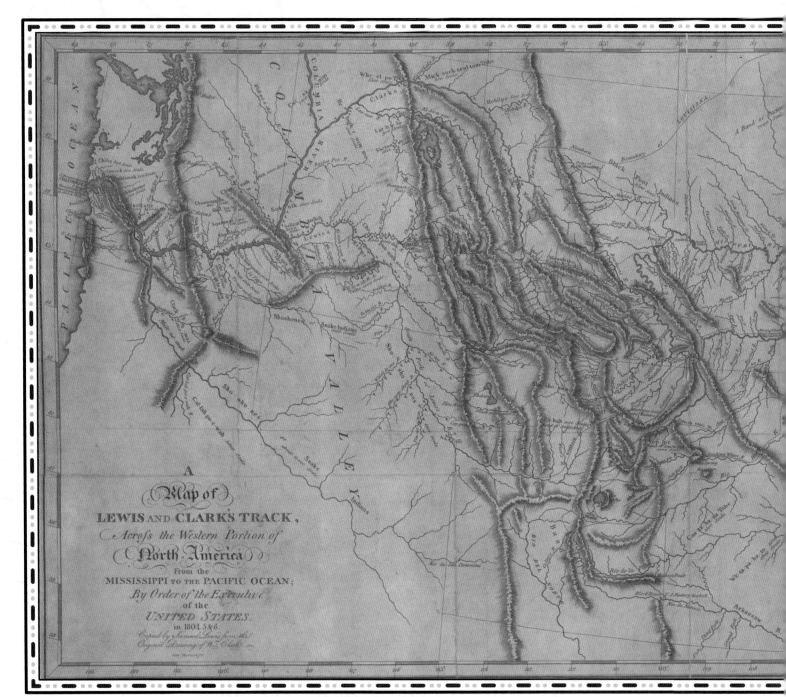

A Map of LEWIS AND CLARK'S TRACK, Across the Western Portion of North America From the MISSISSIPPI TO THE PACIFIC OCEAN; By Order of the Executive of the UNITED STATES, in 1804.5.&6. Copied by Samuel Lewis from the Original Drawing of Wm. Clark.

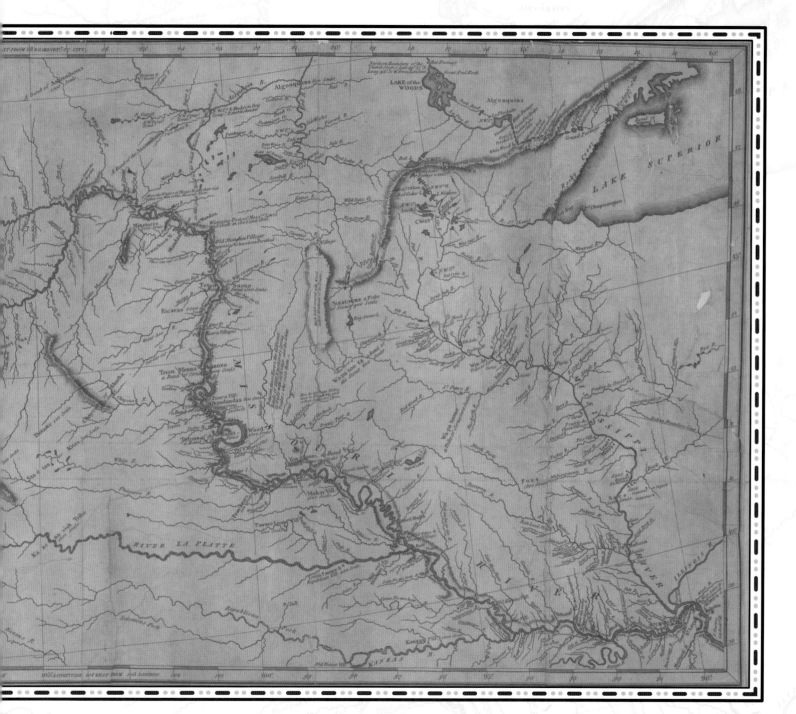

Barbara Fifer is the author of the history portion of *Along the Trail with Lewis and Clark*, and of *Going Along with Lewis & Clark, Day-by-Day With The Lewis & Clark Expedition 1804 to 1806, Wyoming's Historic Forts,* and *Everyday Geography of the United States*.